中译经典文库·语文新课标必读文学名著(双语版)

(生词注解详尽·无障碍阅读)

茶馆

Teahouse

【汉英对照】

老　舍◎著　英若诚◎译

一部蜚声中外的中国戏剧经典

中国出版集团
中国对外翻译出版公司

图书在版编目（CIP）数据

茶馆：汉英对照 / 老舍著；英若诚译. —北京：中国对外翻译出版公司，2008.1

（中译经典文库·语文新课标必读文学名著）

ISBN 978-7-5001-1843-5

Ⅰ. 茶… Ⅱ. ①老… ②英… Ⅲ. ①汉语-英语-对照读物 ②话剧-剧本-中国-现代 Ⅳ. H319.4:I

中国版本图书馆 CIP 数据核字（2007）第 197372 号

出版发行 / 中国对外翻译出版公司
地　　址 / 北京市西城区车公庄大街甲 4 号物华大厦六层
电　　话 /（010）68359376　68359303　68359101　68357937
邮　　编 / 100044
传　　真 /（010）68357870
电子邮箱 / book@ctpc.com.cn
网　　址 / http://www.ctpc.com.cn

总 策 划 / 张高里
执行策划 / 宗　颖　李　虹
责任编辑 / 宗　颖
封面设计 / 大象设计工作室

排　　版 / 北京巴蜀阳光图文设计有限公司
印　　刷 / 北京佳顺印务有限公司
经　　销 / 新华书店

规　　格 / 880 × 1230 毫米　1/32
印　　张 / 6.875
字　　数 / 149 千字
版　　次 / 2008 年 1 月第一版
印　　次 / 2008 年 1 月第一次
印　　数 / 1-5 000

ISBN 978-7-5001-1843-5　　定价：12.00 元

出版说明

多年以来，中国对外翻译出版公司凭借国内一流的翻译和出版实力及资源，精心策划、出版了大批双语读物，在海内外读者中和业界内产生了良好、深远的影响，形成了自己鲜明的出版特色。

二十世纪八九十年代出版的英汉（汉英）对照“一百丛书”，声名远扬，成为一套最权威、最有特色且又实用的双语读物，影响了一代又一代英语学习者和中华传统文化研究者、爱好者；还有“英若诚名剧译丛”、“中华传统文化精粹丛书”、“美丽英文书系”等等，这些优秀的双语读物，有的畅销，有的常销不衰反复再版，有的被选为大学英语阅读教材，受到广大读者的喜爱，获得了良好的社会效益和经济效益。

“语文新课标必读文学名著（双语版）”，是本公司专门为中学生和英语学习者精心打造的又一品牌，是“中译经典文库”的一个新的双语读物系列，具有以下特点：

选题创新——该系列图书是国内第一套为中小学生量身打造的“语文新课标必读文学名著”的双语版读

物，所选篇目均为教育部颁布的语文新课标必读书目或为中学生以及同等文化水平的社会读者喜闻乐见的世界名著，重新编译为英汉（汉英）对照的双语读本。这些书既给青少年读者提供了成长过程中不可或缺的精神食粮，又让他们领略到原著的精髓和魅力，对他们更好地学习英文大有裨益；同时，丛书中入选的《论语》、《茶馆》、《家》等汉英对照读物，亦是热爱中国传统文化的中外读者人所共知的经典名篇，能使读者充分享受阅读经典的无限乐趣。

无障碍阅读——中学生阅读世界文学名著的原著会遇到很多生词和文化难点。针对这一情况，我们给每一篇读物原文中的较难词汇和不易理解之处都加上了注释，在内文的版式设计上也采取英汉（或汉英）对照方式，扫清了学生阅读时的障碍。

优良品质——中译双语读物多年来在读者中享有良好口碑，这得益于作者和出版者对于图书质量的不懈追求。“语文新课标必读文学名著（双语版）”继承了中译双语读物的优良传统——精选的篇目、优秀的译文、方便实用的注解等等，秉承着对每一个读者负责的精神，竭力打造精品图书。

愿这套丛书成为广大读者的良师益友，愿读者在英语学习和传统文化学习两方面都取得新的突破。

人物表

王利发　男，最初与我们见面，他才二十多岁。因父亲早死，他很年轻就做了裕泰茶馆的掌柜。精明，有些自私，而心眼不坏。

唐铁嘴　男，三十来岁。相面为生，吸鸦片。

松二爷　男，三十来岁。胆小而爱说话。

常四爷　男，三十来岁。松二爷的好友，都是裕泰的主顾。正直，体格好。

李　三　男，三十多岁。裕泰跑堂的。勤恳，心眼好。

二德子　男，二十多岁。善扑营当差。

马五爷　男，三十多岁。吃洋教的小恶霸。

刘麻子　男，三十来岁。说媒拉纤，心狠意毒。

康　六　男，四十岁。京郊贫农。

黄胖子　男，四十多岁。流氓头子。

Notes

① act /ækt/ *n.* (剧中的) 幕

② shrewd /ʃruːd/ *a.* 精明的

③ oracle /ˈɔrəkl/ *n.* 神谕，预言

④ fortune-teller *n.* 算命者

⑤ opium /ˈəupjəm/ *n.* 鸦片

⑥ timid /ˈtimid/ *a.* 胆怯的，害羞的

⑦ robust /rəˈbʌst/ *a.* 强壮的，强健的

⑧ imperial /imˈpiəriəl/ *a.* 帝国的

⑨ wrestler /ˈres(ə)lə(r)/ *n.* 摔跤选手

⑩ minor /ˈmainə/ *a.* 次要的，较小的

⑪ live off 依赖……生活

⑫ missionary /ˈmiʃənəri/ *n.* 传教士

⑬ bully /ˈbuli/ *v.* 威胁，恐吓，欺负

⑭ pimp /pimp/ *n.* (美俚)皮条客

⑮ vile /vail/ *a.* 恶劣的

⑯ venomous /ˈvenəməs/ *a.* 恶意的，有毒的

⑰ outskirt /ˈautskəːt/ *n.* 边界，郊外

⑱ tubby /ˈtʌbi/ *a.* 桶状的

DRAMATIS PERSON

Wang Lifa When we first see him, in **Act**[1] One, he is only a little over 20. Though young, he is already the manager of Yutai Teahouse because of his father's early death. A **shrewd**[2] man, somewhat selfish, but not really bad at heart.

Tang The **Oracle**[3] A man around 30, who makes his living by **fortune-telling**[4]. An **opium**[5] addict.

Master Song **Timid**[6] and talkative, in his thirties. Master Ohang A man around 30, upright and **robust**[7], he is a good friend of Song's. Both are regular customers at Yutai Teahouse.

Li San A waiter at Yutai, in his thirties, hard-working and kind-hearted.

Erdez An **Imperial**[8] **Wrestler**[9], in his twenties.

Master Ma A **minor**[10] character, in his thirties, of some influence, who **lives off**[11] the Christian **missionaries**[12] and **bullies**[13] the people.

Pock-Mark Liu A professional **pimp**[14], **vile**[15] and **venomous**[16], in his thirties.

Kang Liu A starving peasant from the **outskirts**[17] of Beijing, about 40 years old.

Tubby[18] Huang An underworld boss, in his forties.

秦仲义 男，王掌柜的房东。在第一幕里二十多岁。阔少，后来成了维新的资本家。

老　人 男，八十二岁。无依无靠。

乡　妇 女，三十多岁。穷得出卖小女儿。

小　妞 女，十岁。乡妇的女儿。

庞太监 男，四十岁。发财之后，想娶老婆。

小牛儿 男，十多岁。庞太监的书童。

宋恩子 男，二十多岁。老式特务。

吴祥子 男，二十多岁。宋恩子的同事。

康顺子 女，在第一幕中十五岁。康六的女儿，被卖给庞太监为妻。

王淑芬 女，四十来岁。王利发掌柜的妻，比丈夫更公平正直些。

巡　警 男，二十多岁。

报　童 男，十六岁。

康大力 男，二十岁。庞太监买来的义子，后与康顺子相依为命。

老　林 男，三十多岁。逃兵。

老　陈 男，三十岁。逃兵，老林的把兄弟。

崔久峰 男，四十多岁。做过国会议员，后来修道，住在裕泰附设的公寓里。

Notes

① premises /ˈpremisiz/ *n.* 房产，房屋

② leaning /ˈliːniŋ/ *n.* 倾斜，倾向

③ destitute /ˈdestitjuːt/ *a.* 困穷的，缺乏

④ eunuch /ˈjuːnək/ *n.* 太监

⑤ amass /əˈmæs/ *v.* 收集，积聚

⑥ foster-mother /ˈfɔstə ˈmʌðə(r)/ *n.* 继母，养母

⑦ attach /əˈtætʃ/ *v.* 附上，使依恋
be attached to 依赖，依靠

⑧ warlord /ˈwɔːlɔːd/ *n.* 军阀

⑨ sworn /swɔːn/ *swear* 的过去分词 *v.* 宣誓，结拜

⑩ devote /diˈvəut/ *v.* 投入于，献身
devote sb. to sth.

Qin Zhongyi Owner of Wang Lira's **premises**①, in his twenties in Act One, son of a rich family. He later becomes a capitalist with Reformist **leanings**②.

Old Man 82 years old, **destitute**③.

Peasant woman In her thirties, so poor that she tries to sell her small daughter.

Little Girl Daughter of the Peasant Woman, 10 years old.

Eunuch④

Eunuch Pang 40 years old, after **amassing**⑤ a fortune, he now wishes to take a wife.

Xiao Niur Pang's personal attendant, in his teens.

Song Enz An old-fashioned secret agent, in his twenties.

Wu Xiangz A colleague of Song Enz, in his twenties.

Kang Shunz Daughter of Kang Liu, 15 years old in Act One, who is sold to Eunuch Pang as his wife.

Wang Shufen Wang Lira's wife, about 40 years old, more fair-minded and upright than her husband.

Policeman In his twenties.

Paper Boy 16 years old.

Kang Dali 20 years old, a son purchased by Eunuch Pang; he and his **foster-mother**⑥ Kang Shunz are deeply **attached**⑦ to each other.

Lao Lin A deserter from the **warlord**⑧ armies, in his thirties.

Lao Chen Another deserter, 30 years old, Lin's **sworn**⑨ brother.

Cui diufeng A former member of parliament, now in his forties, who **devotes**⑩ himself to Buddhist

军　官　男，三十岁。

王大栓　男，四十岁左右。王掌柜的长子，为人正直。

周秀花　女，四十岁。大栓的妻。

王小花　女，十三岁。大栓的女儿。

丁　宝　女，十七岁。女招待，有胆有识。

小刘麻子　男，三十多岁。刘麻子之子，继承父业而发展之。

收电灯费的　男，四十多岁。

小唐铁嘴　男，三十多岁。唐铁嘴之子，继承父业，有做天师的愿望。

明师傅　男，五十多岁。包办酒席的厨师。

邹福远　男，四十多岁。说评书的名手。

卫福喜　男，三十多岁。邹的师弟，先说评书，后改唱京戏。

方　六　男，四十多岁。打小鼓的，奸诈。

Notes

① canonical /kəˈnɔnikəl/ *a.* 依教规的，被认为圣典的

② tenant /ˈtenənt/ *n.* 房客，佃户

③ execution /ˌeksiˈkjuːʃən/ *n.* 处决囚犯

④ squad /skwɔd/ *n.* 班，小队

⑤ virtue /ˈvəːtjuː/ *n.* 美德，优点

⑥ pock-mark /ˈpɔkmɑːk/ *n.* 痘疮，麻点

⑦ KMT abbr. Kuo Min Tang 中国国民党

⑧ superstitious /ˌsjuːpəˈstiʃəs/ *a.* 迷信的

⑨ cult /kʌlt/ *n.* 宗教崇拜者

⑩ chef /ʃef/ *n.* 厨师

⑪ crafty /ˈkrɑːfti/ *a.* 狡猾的

	canonical [1] studies. A **tenant** [2] in the lodging-house attached to Yutai.
Army Officer	30 years old, with the **Execution**[3] **Squad**[4].
Wang Dashuan	Wang Lira's eldest son, about 40 years old, a man ofprinciple.
Zhou Xiuhua	40 years old, Dashuan's wife.
Wang Xiaohua	13-year-old daughter of Dashuan.
Ding Bao	17-year-old waitress of easy **virtue**[5], but with a mind Qf her own and a lot of courage.
Pock-Mark [6] Liu Jr	Son of Pock-mark Liu, in his thirties, carrying on and increasing his father's "profession" .
Electricity Bill Collector	ln his forties.
Tang The Oracle Jr	Son of Tang the Oracle, in his thirties, carrying on his father's profession and entertaining hopes of becoming a Heavenly Teacher in a **KMT**[7]-supported **superstitious**[8] **cult**[9].
Chef Ming	A banquet **chef**[10], in his fifties.
Zou Fuyuan	A well-known professional story-teller, in his forties.
Wei Fuxi	Originally a story-miler trained by the same master as Zou, but now a Beijing opera singer, in his thirties.
Fang Liu	A **crafty**[11] dealer in second-hand goods, in his forties.

车当当 男，三十岁左右。买卖现洋为生。

庞四奶奶 女，四十岁。丑恶，要做皇后。庞太监的四侄媳妇。

春　梅 女，十九岁。庞四奶奶的丫环。

老　杨 男，三十多岁。卖杂货的。

小二德子 男，三十岁。二德子之子，打手。

于厚斋 男，四十多岁。小学教员，王小花的老师。

谢勇仁 男，三十多岁。与于厚斋同事。

小宋恩子 男，三十来岁。宋恩子之子，承袭父业，做特务。

小吴祥子 男，三十来岁。吴祥子之子，世袭特务。

小心眼 女，十九岁。女招待。

沈处长 男，四十岁。宪兵司令部某处处长。

傻　扬 男，数来宝的。

Notes

① repulsive /ri'pʌlsiv/ *a.* 恶心的

② bondmaid /b'ɔndmeid/ *n.* 女仆，女奴

③ pedlar /'pedlə/ *n.* 小贩

④ haberdashery /'hæbədæʃəri/ *n.* 男子服饰，杂货（店）

⑤ thug /θʌg/ *n.* 暴徒，凶残的罪犯

⑥ hereditary /hi'reditəri/ *a.* 世袭的，遗传的

⑦ division /di'viʒən/ *n.* 部门，师（军队里）

⑧ recite /ri'sait/ *v.* 背诵，朗读

⑨ improvised /'imprəvaizd/ *a.* 即席而作的，即兴的

⑩ doggerel /'dɔgərəl/ *n.* 打油诗

Che Dangdang　A dealer in silver dollars, about 30 years old.

Madame Pang　An ugly and **repulsive**① woman of 40, the wife of Eunuch Pang's fourth nephew, and now aspiring to bethe empress of China.

Chunmei　19 years old, **bondmaid**② of Madame Pang.

Yang　**Pedlar**③ of **haberdashery**④, in his thirties.

Erdez Jr　Son of Erdez, and a professional **thug**⑤, 30 years old.

Yu Houzhai　Wang Xiaohua's teacher in the primary school, in hisforties.

Xie Yongren　Another teacher from the same school, in his thirties.

Song Enz Jr　Son of Song Enz, a secret agent like his father, about 30 years old.

Wu Xiangz Jr　Son of Wu Xiangz, a **hereditary**⑥ secret agent, about 30 years old.

Xiao Xinyar　A 19-year-old waitress of easy virtue.

Director Shen　Chief of a **division**⑦ in the Military Police Headquarters, 40 years old.

Silly Yang　A male professional beggar who goes from shop to shop **reciting**⑧ **improvised**⑨ **doggerel**⑩.

茶客若干人　都是男的。

茶房一两个　都是男的。

难民数人　有男有女，有老有少。

公寓住客数人　都是男的。

大兵三五人　都是男的。

押大令的兵七人　都是男的。

宪兵四人　男。

Notes

① lodger /ˈlɔdʒə(r)/ *n.* 寄宿者，投宿者

A number of teahouse customers	all male.
One or two teahouse waiters	all male.
Some refugees	of both sexes and afl ages.
Several **lodgers**①	all male.
Three to five soldiers	all male.
Execution Squad	7 in number, all male.
Four military policemen	all male.

一部蜚声中外的中国戏剧经典

第一幕

时　间　一八九八年（戊戌）初秋，康梁等的维新运动失败了。早半天。

地　点　北京，裕泰大茶馆。

〔幕启：这种大茶馆现在已经不见了。在几十年前，每城都起码有一处。这里卖茶，也卖简单的点心与菜饭。玩鸟的人们，每天在蹓够了画眉、黄鸟等之后，要到这里歇歇腿，喝喝茶，并使鸟儿表演歌唱。商议事情的，说媒拉纤的，也到这里来。那年月，时常有打群架的，但是总会有朋友出头给双方调解；三五十口子打手，经调人东说西说，便都喝碗茶，吃碗烂肉面（大茶馆特殊的食品，价钱便宜，做起来快当），就可以化干戈为玉帛了。总之，这是当日非常重要的地方，有事无事都可以来坐半天。

Notes

① crush /krʌʃ/ *v.* 压碎，征服

② snack /snæk/ *n.* 小吃，点心

③ sufficient /səˈfiʃənt/ *a.* 足够的，充分的

④ stroll /strəul/ *v.* 闲逛，漫步 *stroll about*

⑤ oriole /ˈɔːriəul/ *n.* 金莺类

⑥ thrush /θrʌʃ/ *n.* 画眉

⑦ virtuosity /ˌvəːtjuˈɔsiti/ *n.* 精湛技巧，高超

⑧ transaction /trænˈzækʃən/ *n.* 交易，处理，办理

⑨ haven /ˈheivn/ *n.* 港口，避难所

⑩ tough /tʌf/ *n.* 恶棍

⑪ reconcile /ˈrekənsail/ *v.* 和解，调停

⑫ mediator /ˈmiːdieitə/ *n.* 调解人，中介人

⑬ mince /mins/ *v.* 切碎

ACT 1

Time *Early autumn in 1898, just after the Reform Movement led by Kang Youwei and Liang Qichao had been* **crushed**[①].
Morning.

Place *Yutai Teahouse, Beijing.*

The curtain rises: One doesn't find large teahouses like this any more. A few decades ago, every district in Beijing had at least one. Tea was served as well as simple **snacks**[②] *and quick meals. Bird fanciers, after having spent what they considered* **sufficient**[③] *time* **strolling**[④] *about with their caged* **orioles**[⑤] *and* **thrushes**[⑥], *used to come here every day to rest, sip tea and demonstrate the singing* **virtuosity**[⑦] *of their birds. The teahouse was also a meeting place for all sorts of discussions and* **transactions**[⑧], *and a* **haven**[⑨] *for go-betweens and pimps. Gang figs were common in those days, but fortunately there were always friends around to calm things down. Between 30 to 50* **toughs**[⑩] *from both sides,* **reconciled**[⑪] *through the good offices of a* **mediator**[⑫], *would gather here to drink tea and consume bowls of noodles with* **minced**[⑬] *pork* (*a speciality of large teahouses,*

〔在这里，可以听到最荒唐的新闻，如某处的大蜘蛛怎么成了精，受到雷击。奇怪的意见也在这里可以听到，像把海边上都修上大墙，就足以挡住洋兵上岸。这里还可以听到某京戏演员新近创造了什么腔儿，和煎熬鸦片烟的最好方法。这里也可以看到某人新得到的奇珍——一个出土的玉扇坠儿，或三彩的鼻烟壶。这真是个重要的地方，简直可以算作文化交流的所在。

〔我们现在就要看见这样的一座茶馆。

〔一进门是柜台与炉灶——为省点事，我们的舞台上可以不要炉灶；后面有些锅勺的响声也就够了。屋子非常高大，摆着长桌与方桌，长凳与小凳，都是茶座儿。隔窗可见后院，高搭着凉棚，棚下也有茶座儿。屋里和凉棚下都有挂鸟笼的地方。各处都贴着"莫谈国事"的纸条。

Notes

① while away *v.* 消磨（度过）

② preposterous /pri'pɔstərəs/ *a.* 荒谬的，可笑的

③ demon /'diːmən/ *n.* 魔鬼

④ expedient /iks'piːdiənt/ *n.* 权宜之计，临时手段

⑤ aria /'ɑː riə/ *n.* 抒情调，独唱曲

⑥ excavate /'ekskəveit/ *v.* 挖开，凿通

⑦ fan pendant /'pendənt/ *n.* 垂饰

⑧ glaze /gleiz/ *v.* 上釉，变为光滑

⑨ snuff-box *n.* 鼻烟壶

⑩ counter /'kauntə/ *n.* 柜台

⑪ stove /stəuv/ *n.* 炉子

⑫ clatter /'klætə/ *n.* 撞击声，哗啦声

⑬ rectangular /rek'tæŋgjulə/ *n.* 矩形

⑭ stool /stuːl/ *n.* 凳子，搁脚凳

⑮ matted /'mætid/ *a.* 铺席子的

⑯ canopy /'kænəpi/ *n.* 天篷，遮篷

cheap and easy to prepare], and peace would once more have been restored in the land. In short, the teahouse was a most important institution, a place where people could come for business or just to **while away**[1] *the time.*

At its tables one could hear the most **preposterous**[2] *stories, such as how a giant spider turned into a* **demon**[3] *until it was finally struck by ligning; or the most extraordinary views, such as how far it was possible to prevent all foreign armies from landing by the simple* **expedient**[4] *of building a long high wall along the seacoast. Yet this was also the place to learn the latest* **aria**[5] *devised by some Beijing opera actor or the most sophisticated method for preparing opium. Here too one could see newly-acquired treasures such as an* **excavated**[6] *jade* **fan pendant**[7] *or a three-colour* **glazed**[8] **snuff-box**[9]*. The teahouse was indeed an important place, almost a centre of cultural exchange.*

It is just such a teahouse we are about to see.

Immediately inside the entrance we see the **counter**[10] *and the brick* **stove**[11]*, though for the stage we can do away with the stove if it's too much trouble and make do with the* **clatter**[12] *of pots and pans offstage. The building is extremely large and high, with* **rectangular**[13] *tables, square tables, benches and* **stools**[14] *for the customers. Through the window an inner courtyard can be seen, where there is a* **matted**[15] **canopy**[16] *for shade and seats for customers. There are devices for hanging up bird-cages, both in the teahouse and in the courtyard. Paper slips, with "Do not discuss*

〔有两位茶客，不知姓名，正眯着眼，摇着头，拍板低唱。有两三位茶客，也不知姓名，正入神地欣赏瓦罐里的蟋蟀。两位穿灰色大衫的——宋恩子与吴祥子，正低声地谈话，看样子他们是北衙门的办案的（侦缉）。

〔今天又有一起打群架的，据说是为了争一只家鸽，惹起非用武力解决不可的纠纷。假若真打起来，非出人命不可，因为被约的打手中包括着善扑营的哥儿们和库兵，身手都十分厉害。好在，不能真打起来，因为在双方还没把打手约齐，已有人出面调停了——现在双方在这里会面。三三两两的打手，都横眉立目，短打扮，随时进来，往后院去。

〔马五爷在不惹人注意的角落，独

① slit /slit/ *n.* 裂缝，细缝
② hum /hʌm/ *v.* 发低哼声，闭口哼歌
③ fascinate /ˈfæsineit/ *v.* 令人入神，使……入迷
④ gown /gaun/ *n.* 长袍，长外衣
⑤ deduce /diˈdjuːs/ *v.* 推论，演绎出
⑥ brew /bruː/ *v.* 酿造，蕴酿
⑦ prowess /ˈpraʊis/ *n.* 英勇，勇敢
⑧ ranks /ræŋk/ *n.* 队伍
⑨ bring about *v.* 带来，发生，引起
⑩ truce /truːs/ *n.* 休战
⑪ belligerent /biˈlidʒərənt/ *a.* 好战的，交战的
⑫ inconspicuously /ˌinkənˈspikjuəsli/ *ad.* 不显眼地，难以觉察地

affairs of state" written on them, are pasted all over the place.

Two customers, who shall be nameless, with their eyes narrowed to a **slit**① and their heads rocking, are softly **humming**② a tune, beating time with their hands. Two or three others, also nameless, are **fascinated**③ by some crickets in an earthenware jar. Two menin grey **gowns**④, Song Enz and Wu Xiangz, are talking to each otherin whispers. From their appearance one can **deduce**⑤ they are agents from the Northern Yamen, the security authority in those days.

Another gang fig has been **brewing**⑥ today. The reason, according to some sources, was a dispute over the ownership of a pigeon. It seemed quite likely that the whole affair mig end in violence. If so, then a loss of life would result, for the toughs invited by both parties included characters well-known for their physical **prowess**⑦ such as the Imperial Wrestlers and Guards of the Imperial Storehouses. Fortunately, nothing of the sort will happen, for before either party had assembled their **ranks**⑧, mediators were already busy trying to **bring about**⑨ some kind of **truce**⑩ so now, the two sides are meeting in the teahouse. Throughout the first part of this act these toughs, in twos and threes, looking **belligerent**⑪ and dressed in short clothes 〔for figing, as opposed to long gowns〕, will enter the teahouse and head for the inner courtyard.

Master Ma, alone in a corner, sits **inconspicuously**⑫

自坐着喝茶。

〔王利发高高地坐在柜台里。

〔唐铁嘴趿拉着鞋，身穿一件极长极脏的大布衫，耳上夹着几张小纸片，进来。

王利发 唐先生，你外边蹓蹓吧！

唐铁嘴 （惨笑）王掌柜，捧捧唐铁嘴吧！送给我碗茶喝，我就先给您相相面吧！手相奉送，不取分文！（不容分说，拉过王利发的手来）今年是光绪二十四年，戊戌。您贵庚是……

王利发 （夺回手去）算了吧，我送给你一碗茶喝，你就甭卖那套生意口啦！用不着相面，咱们既在江湖内，都是苦命人！（由柜台内走出，让唐铁嘴坐下）坐下！我告诉你，你要是不戒了大烟，就永远交不了好运！这是我的相法，比你的更灵验！

〔松二爷和常四爷都提着鸟笼进来，

Notes

① vantage /ˈvɑːntidʒ/ *n.* 优势，有利情况

② tuck /tʌk/ *v.* 卷起，挤进

③ temple /ˈtempl/ *n.*太阳穴

④ wan /wɔn/ *a.* 苍白的，有病的

⑤ boost up 鼓励，激励

⑥ throw in 附送

⑦ copper /ˈkɔpə/ *n.* 铜，铜币

⑧ reign /rein/ *n.* 执政，王朝

⑨ snatch /snætʃ/ *v.* 夺取，想抢走

⑩ spare /spɛə/ *v.*节约，省去

⑪ harsh /hɑːʃ/ *a.* 残酷的，无情的

drinking tea.

Wang Lifa sits at a **vantage**[①]*-point behind the counter.*

Tang the Oracle enters, his shoes half off his feet, and wearing an extremely long and dirty gown, some scraps of paper **tucked**[②] *into his hat near the* **temples**[③].

Wang Lifa Mr Tang, why not take a walk somewhere else?

Tang the oracle [*with a* **wan**[④] *smile*] Oh, Manager Wang, **boost up**[⑤] poor old Oracle a bit. Offer me a cup of tea, and I'll tell your fortune for you. With palm-readin **thrown in**[⑥], it won't cost you a **copper**[⑦]! [*Without waiting for Wang's consent, takes hold of his! hand.*] Now, it's the 24th year of Emperor Guangxu's **reign**[⑧], the Year of the Dog, and your honourable age...?

Wang Lifa [***snatching***[⑨] *his hand away*] Enough, enough! I'll give you a cup of tea, but **spare**[⑩] me the sales talk. What's the point of fortune-telling? In this **harsh**[⑪] world, we're all on our own. Life will never be easy. [*Comes out from behind the counter and makes Tang sit down.*] Sit down! Listen! If you don't stop smoking opium, you'll never have any luck. There, you see, I'm a better fortune-teller than you!

[*Master Song and Master Chang enter, each*

王利发向他们打招呼。他们先把鸟笼子挂好，找地方坐下。松二爷文诌诌的，提着小黄鸟笼；常四爷雄赳赳的，提着大而高的画眉笼。茶房李三赶紧过来，沏上盖碗茶。他们自带茶叶。茶沏好，松二爷、常四爷向邻近的茶座让了让。

松二爷
常四爷 您喝这个！（然后，往后院看了看）

松二爷 好像又有事儿？

常四爷 反正打不起来！要真打的话，早到城外头去啦；到茶馆来干吗？

〔二德子，一位打手，恰好进来，听见了常四爷的话。

二德子 （凑过去）你这是对谁甩闲话呢？

常四爷 （不肯示弱）你问我哪？花钱喝茶，难道还教谁管着吗？

松二爷 （打量了二德子一番）我说这位爷，您是营里当差的吧？来，坐下喝一碗，我们也都是外场人。

二德子 你管我当差不当差呢！

常四爷 要抖威风，跟洋人干去，洋人厉

Notes

① genteel /dʒen'tiːl/ *a.* 文雅的，有教养的

② sturdy /'stəːdi/ *a.* 强健的，健全的

③ dimension /di'menʃən/ *n.* 尺寸，容积

④ lidded /'lidid/ *a.* 有盖子的

⑤ blow /bləu/ *n.* 打击，殴打

⑥ overhear /ˌəuvə'hiə/ *v.* 无意中听到，偷听

⑦ intimidate /in'timideit/ *v.* 威胁，恐吓，胁迫

⑧ size up *n.* 估量，估计

⑨ throw one's weight around 滥用权势，耀武扬威

carrying a bird-cage. Greeted by Wang Lifa, they hang up the cages, then look for a place to sit. Song, who has a **genteel**[①] *air about him, carries a delicate oriole's cage, whereas Chang, looking bold and* **sturdy**[②], *has with him a thrush's cage of much greater* **dimensions**[③]. *The waiter Li San hurries over to prepare their* **lidded**[④] *cups of tea, the leaves of which they have broug themselves. When the tea is ready, Song and Chang offer it to the customers around them.*〕

Master Song / Master Chang Won't you have some of this?〔*They look towards nner courtyard.*〕

Song Trouble again?

Chang Don't worry, they won't come to **blows**[⑤]. If it was serious, they'd have gone out of the city long before this. Why come to a teahouse?

〔*Erdez, one of the toughs, enters just in time to* **overhear**[⑥] *Chang's words.*〕

Erdez 〔*moving over*〕 What you think you're talking about?

Chang 〔*refusing to be* **intimidated**[⑦]〕 Who, me? I've paid for my tea. Do I have to bow to anyone too?

Song 〔*after* **sizing up**[⑧] *Erdez*〕 Excuse me, sir, you serve in the Imperial Wrestlers, don't you? Come, sit down. Let's have a cup of tea together. We're all men of the world.

Erdez Where I serve ain't none of your bloody business!

Chang If you want to **throw your weight around**[⑨], try the

害！英法联军烧了圆明园。尊家吃着官饷，可没见您去冲锋打仗！

二德子 甭说打洋人不打，我先管教管教你！（要动手）

〔别的茶客依旧进行他们自己的事。王利发 急忙跑过来。

王利发 哥们儿，都是街面上的朋友，有话好说，德爷，您后边坐！

〔二德子不听王利发的话，一下子把一个盖碗搂下桌去，摔碎。翻手要抓常四爷的脖领。

常四爷 （闪过）你要怎么着？

二德子 怎么着？我碰不了洋人，还碰不了你吗？

马五爷 （并未立起）二德子，你威风啊！

二德子 （四下扫视，看到马五爷）喝，马五爷，您在这儿哪？我可眼拙，没看见您！（过去请安）

马五爷 有什么事好好地说，干吗动不动地就讲打？

二德子 嗻！您说得对！我到后头坐坐去。李三，这儿的茶钱我候啦！（往后

① alright /ˌɔːl'rait/ *ad.* 毫无疑问

② payroll /'peirəul/ *n.* 工资单

③ raze /reiz/ *v.* 消除，破坏

④ unperturbed /'ʌnpə'təːbd/ *a.* 未受到搅乱的，平静的

⑤ smash /smæʃ/ *v.* 粉碎，溃裂

⑥ grab /græb/ *v.* 抓取，抢去

⑦ dodge /dɔdʒ/ *v.* 避开，躲避

⑧ obeisance /əu'beisns/ *n.* 鞠躬，敬礼

⑨ resort to 诉诸，求助于

⑩ fisticuffs /'fistikʌfs/ *n.* 互殴，乱斗

foreigners! They're tough **alright**[1]! You're on the public **payroll**[2], but when the British and the French armies **razed**[3] the old Summer Palace, I didn't see you lift a finger to stop them!

Erdez Leave the foreigners out of this! I'll teach you a lesson first! 〔*Raises his fist.*〕

〔*The other customers go about their business* **unperturbed**[4]. *Wang Lifa, however, rushes over.*〕

Wang Lifa Now, now, gentlemen! Surely we can settle this as friends. Master Erdez, why not take a seat in the inner courtyard now?

〔*Erdez, ignoring Wang Lifa, suddenly sweeps a teacup off the table,* **smashing**[5] *it. He makes a move, trying to* **grab**[6] *Chang by the collar.*〕

Chang 〔**dodging**[7] *him*〕 What do you think you're doing?

Erdez Perhaps I don't touch the foreigners, but I'll give you one of me touches. I will!

Master ma 〔*without getting up*〕 Erdez, you're quite an important person, aren't you?

Erdez 〔*looking round and spotting Ma*〕 Oh, it's you, Master Ma! Pardon, sir, I never see'd you sitting there. 〔*Goes over to Ma, dropping one knee in the traditional gesture of* **obeisance**[8].〕

Master ma Settle your disputes in a reasonable way. Must you always **resort to**[9] **fisticuffs**[10]?

Erdez Yes, sir. I'll go direct to the inner courtyard. Li San, I'm paying for this table! 〔*Exit to inner courtyard.*〕

面走去)

常四爷 (凑过来，要对马五爷发牢骚) 这位爷，您圣明，您给评评理!

马五爷 (立起来) 我还有事，再见! (走出去)

常四爷 (对王利发) 邪! 这倒是个怪人!

王利发 您不知道这是马五爷呀! 怪不得您也得罪了他!

常四爷 我也得罪了他? 我今天出门没挑好日子!

王利发 (低声地) 刚才您说洋人怎样，他就是吃洋饭的。信洋教，说洋话，有事情可以一直地找宛平县的县太爷去，要不怎么连官面上都不惹他呢!

常四爷 (往原处走) 哼，我就不佩服吃洋饭的!

王利发 (向宋恩子、吴祥子那边稍一歪头，低声地) 说话请留点神! (大声地) 李三，再给这儿沏一碗来! (拾起地上的碎瓷片)

松二爷 盖碗多少钱? 我赔! 外场人不做老娘们事!

王利发 不忙，待会儿再算吧! (走开)

〔纤手刘麻子领着康六进来。刘麻子先向松二爷、常四爷打招呼。

Notes

① air /ɛə/ *v.* 宣扬，显示
② grievance /ˈgriːvəns/ *n.* 委屈，冤情

③ snub /snʌb/ *v.* 冷落，不理睬
④ offend /əˈfend/ *v.* 犯罪，冒犯

⑤ mayor /mɛə/ *n.* 市长

⑥ tilt /tilt/ *v.* (使) 倾斜

⑦ shard /ʃɑːd/ *n.* 碎片

Chang 〔*coming over to Ma, wishing to* ***air***① *his* ***grievances***②〕 Sir, you're a sensible gentleman. Pleasetell us who you think was rig?

Master ma 〔*standing up*〕I'm busy. Goodbye! 〔*Exit.*〕

Chang 〔*to Wang Lifa*〕How odd! Queer character, isn't he?

Wang Lifa Don't you know that's Master Ma? No wonder he **snubbed**③ you. You **offended**④ him too.

Chang Offended him? This is my lucky day!

Wang Lifa 〔*lowering his voice*〕 You were saying something about foreigners just now. Well, he lives off the foreigners. Follows their religion and speaks their language. If he wants he can go straig to the **Mayor**⑤ of Beijing on business. That's why even the authorities handle him with care.

Chang 〔*going back to his seat*〕 Pshaw! I've no time for people who serve foreign masters!

Wang Lifa 〔***tilting***⑥ *his head sligly in the direction of Song Enz and Wu Xiangz, in a whisper*〕 Be careful what you say! 〔*In a louder voice*〕 Li San, a fresh cup of tea here! 〔*Picks up the* ***shards***⑦ *of the smashed teacup.*〕

Song How much for that teacup? I'll pay for it. We men aren't like mean old women!

Wang Lifa No hurry. We can settle that later. 〔*Moves off.*〕

〔*The pimp Pock-mark Liu leads Kang Liu in. First, Pock-mark Liu greets Song and Chang.*〕

刘麻子 您二位真早班儿！（掏出鼻烟壶，倒烟）您试试这个！刚装来的，地道英国造，又细又纯！

常四爷 唉！连鼻烟也得从外洋来！这得往外流多少银子啊！

刘麻子 咱们大清国有的是金山银山，永远花不完！您坐着，我办点小事！（领康六找了个座儿）

〔李三拿过一碗茶来。

刘麻子 说说吧，十两银子行不行？你说干脆的！我忙，没工夫专伺候你！

康　六 刘爷！十五岁的大姑娘，就值十两银子吗？

刘麻子 卖到窑子去，也许多拿一两八钱的，可是你又不肯！

康　六 那是我的亲女儿！我能够……

刘麻子 有女儿，你可养活不起，这怪谁呢？

康　六 那不是因为乡下种地的都没法子混了吗？一家大小要是一天能吃上一顿粥，我要还想卖女儿，我就不是人！

刘麻子 那是你们乡下的事，我管不着。我受你之托，教你不吃亏，又教你女儿有个吃饱饭的地方，这还不好吗？

Notes

① measure out 量出
② genuine /'dʒenjuin/ *a.* 真正的，真实的
③ run out 用尽，耗尽
④ tael /teil/ *n.* 两
⑤ brothel /'brɔθəl/ *n.* 妓院
⑥ gruel /gruəl/ *n.* 稀粥

Pock-markliu You gentlemen are early today. 〔*Takes out a snuff-box and* **measure out**① *a little.*〕 You must try this! I just got it, the **genuine**② thing from England! So fine and pure!

Chang Imagine! Even our snuff has to come from abroad. How much silver must flow out of the country every year!

Pock-markliu Our Great Qing Empire has mountains of silver and gold. It'll never **run out**③. Please be seated, I've some business to attend to. 〔*Leads Kang Liu to a seat.*〕

〔*Li San brings over a cup of tea.*〕

Pock-markliu Now, let's talk it over. Will ten **taels**④ of silver do? Be quick! I'm a busy man. I haven't got all day to wait on you!

Kang Liu Master Liu! A fifteen-year-old girl only worth ten taels?

Pock-markliu A **brothel**⑤ mig give you a few taels more, but you don't want that.

Kang Liu My flesh and blood, how could I... ?

Pock-markliu But you can't feed her. Who's to blame?

Kang Liu We peasants can't live any more. If we had a bowl of **gruel**⑥ each every day...and I still wanted to sell my dauger, then I'd be a beast!

Pock-markliu That's your problem, not mine! You asked me to help you, so I'll see to it you're not cheated and your dauger fills her belly. What more do you

康　六　到底给谁呢?

刘麻子　我一说，你必定从心眼里乐意！一位在宫里当差的!

康　六　宫里当差的谁要个乡下丫头呢?

刘麻子　那不是你女儿的命好吗?

康　六　谁呢?

刘麻子　庞总管！你也听说过庞总管吧？侍候着太后，红的不得了，连家里打醋的瓶子都是玛瑙做的!

康　六　刘大爷，把女儿给太监做太婆，我怎么对得起人呢?

刘麻子　卖女儿，无论怎么卖，也对不起女儿！你糊涂！你看，姑娘一过门，吃的是珍馐美味，穿的是绫罗绸缎，这不是造化吗？怎样，摇头不算点头算，来个干脆的!

康　六　自古以来，哪有……他就给十两银子?

刘麻子　找遍了你们全村儿，找得出十两银子找不出？在乡下，五斤白面就换个孩子，你不是不知道!

康　六　我，唉！我得跟姑娘商量一下!

刘麻子　告诉你，过了这个村可没有这个店，耽误了事别怨我！快去快来!

① dowager /ˈdauədʒə/ *n.* 继承亡夫爵位（或遗产的）遗孀，贵妇

② vinegar /ˈvinigə/ *n.* 醋

③ agate /ˈægət/ *n.* 玛瑙

④ brocade /brəˈkeid/ *n.* 织锦

⑤ scrape up 凑集积蓄，积攒

⑥ catty /ˈkæti/ *n.* 斤

want?

Kang Liu Who's she being sold to?

Pock-markliu This should please you. A palace official!

Kang Liu What palace official wants a peasant girl?

Pock-markliu That's why your dauger's a lucky girl!

Kang Liu But who is he?

Pock-markliu The Grand Eunuch Pang! Even you must have heard of him. A personal attendant of the Empress **Dowager**①, her great favourite! Even the **vinegar**② bottle in his house is made of **agate**③!

Kang Liu But Master Liu, please, how could I ever face my dauger again if I sold her to be the wife of a eunuch?

Pock-markliu But you are selling her, aren't you? How can you face her any way? Don't be afool! Think about it. Once she's married, she'll eat delicacies and wear **brocades**④! I call that a lucky fate! Well, make up your mind, yes or no. Let's get it over with!

Kang Liu But who's ever heard of such a thing...? Ten taels. Is that all he'll pay?

Pock-markliu Where in your whole village can you **scrape up**⑤ ten taels? You know very well in the countryside a child can be boug for five **catties**⑥ of wheat flour.

Kang Liu I, well, I'll have to talk it over with my dauger.

Pock-markliu I'm telling you, you won't find another chance like this. If you lose it, don't blame me! You'd better get a move on.

康　六　唉！我一会儿就回来！

刘麻子　我在这儿等着你！

〔康六慢慢地走出去。

刘麻子　（凑到松二爷、常四爷这边来）乡下人真难办事，永远没有个痛痛快快！

松二爷　这号生意又不小吧？

刘麻子　也甜不到哪儿去，弄好了，赚个元宝！

常四爷　乡下是怎么了，会弄得这么卖儿卖女的！

刘麻子　谁知道！要不怎么说，就是一条狗也得托生在北京城里嘛！

常四爷　刘爷，您可真有个狠劲儿，给拉拢这路事！

刘麻子　我要不分心，他们还许找不到买主呢！（忙岔话）松二爷（掏出个小时表来），您看这个！

松二爷　（接表）好体面的小表！

刘麻子　您听听，嘎登嘎登地响！

松二爷　（听）这得多少钱？

刘麻子　您爱吗？就让给你！一句话，五两银子！您玩够了，不爱再要了，我还照数退钱！东西真地道，传家的玩艺！

常四爷　我这儿正嘀摸这个味儿：咱们一个人

Notes

① drag /dræg/ v. 拖累，拖拉

② bumpkin /'bʌmpkin/ n. 粗人，乡巴佬

③ nuisance /'njuːsns/ n. 讨厌的东西，讨厌的人

④ make up one's mind 做出决定，下定决心

⑤ nerve /nəːv/ n. 精神，勇气

⑥ abruptly /ə'brʌptli/ ad. 突然地

⑦ tick away （时间一分一秒地）过去

⑧ refund /riː'fʌnd/ v. 付还，偿还借款

⑨ heirloom /'eəluːm/ n. 传家宝

Kang Liu Yes. I'll be back as soon as I can.

Pock-markliu I'll be here waiting for you.

〔*Exit Kang Liu*, **dragging**① *his feet.*〕

Pock-markliu 〔*moving over to Song and Chang*〕 These country **bumpkins** ② are a **nuisance** ③. They're so slow **making up their minds**④!

Song Another big deal?

Pock-markliu Not so big. If all goes well, I may get about twenty taels of silver.

Chang What's going on in the countryside? Why are they selling their children like this?

Pock-markliu Who knows? That's why people say, even a dog wants to be born in Beijing.

Chang Master Liu, it takes **nerve**⑤ to have a hand in such a business!

Pock-markliu But if I didn't bother, they mig not find a buyer! 〔*Changing the subject* ***abruptly*** ⑥〕 Master Song 〔*taking a small pocket-watch out of his pocket*〕, have a look at this!

Song 〔*taking the watch*〕What a fine little watch!

Pock-markliu Listen to it, **ticking away**⑦ merrily!

Song 〔*listening*〕 How much does it cost?

Pock-markliu Why, you like it? Then it's yours! Just five taels! Whenever you're tired of it, give it back to me and I'll **refund**⑧ you to the last copper! It's really top quality, fit for a family **heirloom**⑨.

Chang It puzzles me, the amount of foreign thing we all

身上有多少洋玩艺儿啊！老刘，就看你身上吧：洋鼻烟，洋表，洋缎大衫，洋布裤褂……

刘麻子 洋东西可真是漂亮呢！我要是穿一身土布，像个乡下脑壳，谁还理我呀！

常四爷 我老觉乎着咱们的大缎子，川绸，更体面！

刘麻子 松二爷，留下这个表吧，这年月，戴着这么好的洋表，会教人另眼看待！是不是这么说，您哪？

松二爷 (真爱表，但又嫌贵) 我……

刘麻子 您先戴两天，改日再给钱！

〔黄胖子进来。

黄胖子 (严重的沙眼，看不清楚，进门就请安) 哥儿们，都瞧我啦！我请安了！都是自已弟兄，别伤了和气呀！

王利发 这不是他们，他们在后院哪！

黄胖子 我看不大清楚啊！掌柜的，预备烂肉面，有我黄胖子，谁也打不起来！ (往里走)

二德子 (出来迎接) 两边已经见了面，您快来

Notes

① satin /'sætin/ *n.* 缎子

② clodhopper /'klɔdhɔpə (r) / *n.* 〈口〉庄稼汉，乡巴佬

③ trachoma /trə'kəumə/ *n.* 砂眼

④ head for 取向于，前往

have. Take you, for instance, Liu, you have foreign snuff, a foreign watch, a gown made from foreign **satin**①, and a jacket and trousers made of foreign cloth...

Pock-markliu But foreign things look so fine! If I went around in country cloth, looking like a **clodhopper**②, who'd ever talk to me?

Chang I still think our own satin and Sichuan silk are more handsome.

Pock-markliu Master Song, you really oug to keep this watch. Nowadays, if you carry a foreign watch around, people will treat you with new respect. Isn't that so?

Song 〔*in love with the watch, but shying at the price*〕I...

Pock-markliu Keep it for the time being. You can pay later!

〔*Tubby Huang enters.*〕

Tubby Huang 〔*a severe case of* ***trachoma***③, *with consequently very poor eyesig. Bending one knee as soon as he enters*〕Now, now, folks, for my sake, please, I'm here greetin' you all! We're all brothers, ain't we? Let's have none of them bad feelings!

Wang Lifa These aren't the people you've come to see. They're in the inner courtyard.

Tubby Huang Oh, my sig ain't too good! Manager Wang, prepare them bowls of noodles! With me, Tubby Huang here, no one's goin' to fig! 〔***Heads for***④ *the inner courtyard.*〕

Erdez 〔*coming out to greet him*〕The two sides have already

吧!

〔二德子同黄胖子入内。

〔茶房们一趟又一趟地往后面送茶水。老人进来，拿着些牙签、胡梳、耳挖勺之类的小东西，低着头慢慢地挨着茶座儿走；没人买他的东西。他要往后院去，被李三截住。

李　三　老大爷，您外边蹓蹓吧！后院里，人家正说和事呢，没人买您的东西！（顺手儿把剩茶递给老人一碗）

松二爷　（低声地）李三！（指后院）他们到底为了什么事，要这么拿刀动杖的？

李　三　（低声地）听说是为一只鸽子，张宅的鸽子飞到了李宅去，李宅不肯交还……唉，咱们还是少说话好，（问老人）老大爷您高寿啦？

老　人　（喝了茶）多谢！八十二了，没人管！这年月呀，人还不如一只鸽子呢！唉！（慢慢走出去）

〔秦仲义，穿得很讲究，满面春风，走进来。

王利发　哎哟！秦二爷，您怎么这样闲在，会想

Notes

① earpick /'iəpik/ *n.* 耳挖

② ware /wɛə/ *n.* 器具，货物

③ left-over /'left.əuvə/ *n.* 残留物，剩饭

④ spoil for 心想

⑤ meticulously /me'tikjuləsli/ *ad.* 过分注意细节的，谨小慎微的

met. Come quick!

〔*Erdez and Tubby Huang go in.*〕

〔*Waiters begin to busy themselves taking hot water for tea into the inner courtyard. The Old Man, carrying metal toothpicks, beard combs,* **earpicks**① *and such items, enters. He moves slowly from table to table, his head bent. No one is interested in his* **wares**②. *Just as he is heading for the inner courtyard, he is stopped by Li San.*〕

Li San Now, old uncle, better try somewhere else. They're trying to settle a dispute in there. No one will buy your things. 〔*Hands him a cup of* **left-over**③ *tea in passing.*〕

Song 〔*lowering his voice*〕 Li San! 〔*Pointing at the inner courtyard*〕 What's it all about? Why are they **spoiling for**④ a fig?

Li San 〔*in a low voice*〕 It's supposed to be all over a pigeon, which flew from the Zhang family over to the Lis. The Lis refused to return it... Well, better not go into it. 〔*To the Old Man*〕 Old uncle, you must be well on in years.

Old man 〔*drinking the tea*〕 Thanks a lot. I'm eigy-two! No one to look after me. These days, a pigeon's better off than a man. Well, well! 〔*Goes out slowly.*〕

〔*Qin Zhongyi,* **meticulously**⑤ *dressed and in high spirits, enters.*〕

Wang Lifa Oh! Master Qin! How can you spare the time to

起下茶馆来了？也没带个底下人？

秦仲义 来看看，看看你这年轻小伙子会作生意不会！

王利发 唉，一边做一边学吧，指着这个吃饭嘛。谁叫我爸爸死得早，我不干不行啊！好在照顾主儿都是我父亲的老朋友，我有不周到的地方，都肯包涵，闭闭眼就过去了。在街面上混饭吃，人缘儿顶要紧。我按着我父亲遗留下的老办法，多说好话，多请安，讨人人的喜欢，就不会出大岔子！您坐下，我给您沏碗小叶茶去！

秦仲义 我不喝，也不坐着！

王利发 坐一坐！有您在我这儿坐坐，我脸上有光！

秦仲义 也好吧！（坐）可是，用不着奉承我！

王利发 李三，沏一碗高的来！二爷，府上都好？您的事情都顺心吧？

秦仲义 不怎么太好！

王利发 您怕什么呢？那么多的买卖，您的小手指头都比我的腰还粗！

唐铁嘴 （凑过来）这位爷好相貌，真是天庭饱满，地阁方圆，虽无宰相之权，而有

Notes

① accompany /ə'kʌmpəni/ *v.* 陪伴，带有

② overlook /ˌəuvə'luk/ *v.* 忽视，没注意到

③ slip /slip/ *n.* 滑，错误

④ make a fuss 大惊小怪，吵吵闹闹

⑤ choice /tʃɔis/ *a.* 上等的，精选的

⑥ thriving /'θraiviŋ/ *a.* 成功的，旺盛的

⑦ mere /miə/ *a.* 纯粹的，仅仅的

⑧ trifle /'traifl/ *n.* 琐事，少量

⑨ edge /edʒ/ *v.* 侧身移动，挤进

⑩ auspicious /ɔː'spiʃəs/ *n.* 吉兆的，幸运的

⑪ forehead /'fɔrid/ *n.* 额，前额

visit the teahouse? Not even a servant to **accompany**[1] you?

Qin Zhongyi Just taking a look around — to see if a young fellow like you can run a business like this.

Wang Lifa Well, I learn as I go along. I have to. It's my living! With my father dying so young, I've no choice. Luckily my customers were all friends of my father. They're ready to **overlook**[2] my **slips**[3]. In a business like this you have to be popular. I do everything just like my father. Always be polite, always make obeisances, try to please everybody. Then there won't be any serious trouble. Please take a seat, sir. I'll make you a cup of our very best tea.

Qin Zhongyi I don't want any tea and I won't sit down.

Wang Lifa Just for a moment! You'll be doing me a great honour.

Qin Zhongyi Oh, all rig. 〔*Sits.*〕 But don't **make such a fuss**[4].

Wang Lifa Li San, a cup of our **choicest**[5] tea. Sir, your family are all well, I hope? And what about your business? **Thriving**[6]?

Qin Zhongyi Not so good.

Wang Lifa But surely you've got nothing to worry about. With so m; ny different interests, a **mere**[7] **trifle**[8] to you would be my entire fortune and more!

Tang the oracle 〔***edging***[9] *his way closer*〕 Oh, what **auspicious**[10] features! Truly an inspired **forehead**[11] and a

陶朱之富!

秦仲义　躲开我!去!

王利发　先生，你喝够了茶，该外边活动活动去!（把唐铁嘴轻轻推开）

唐铁嘴　唉!（垂头走出去）

秦仲义　小王，这儿的房租是不是得往上提那么一提呢?当年你爸爸给我的那点租钱，还不够我喝茶用的呢!

王利发　二爷，您说得对，太对了!可是，这点小事用不着您分心，您派管事的来一趟，我跟他商量，该长多少租钱，我一定照办!是!喳!

秦仲义　你这小子，比你爸爸还滑!哼，等着吧，早晚我把房子收回去!

王利发　您甭吓唬着我玩，我知道您多么照应我，心疼我，决不会叫我挑着大茶壶，到街上卖热茶去!

秦仲义　你等着瞧吧!

〔乡妇拉着个十来岁的小妞进来。小妞的头上插着一根草标。李三本想不许她们往前走，可是心中一难过，没管。

Notes

① jaw /dʒɔː/ *n.* 颚，颌

② potential /pəˈtenʃ(ə)l/ *n.* 潜力，潜能

③ fabulous /ˈfæbjuləs/ *a.* 传说的，难以置信的

④ dejectedly /diˈdʒektidli/ *ad.* 沮丧地，萎靡地

⑤ pittance /ˈpitəns/ *n.* 少量，施舍少量的钱

⑥ steward /ˈstjuəd/ *n.* 管家，管事

⑦ rogue /rəug/ *n.* 流氓

⑧ straw /strɔː/ *n.* 稻草，麦杆

commanding **jaw**[1]! Not the makings of a prime minister, but the **potentials**[2] of **fabulous**[3] wealth!

Qin Zhongyi Leave me alone. Go away!

Wang Lifa Mr Tang, you've had your tea, go somewhere else. 〔*Gently pushes Tang away.*〕

Tang the oracle Oh, very well! 〔*Exit* ***dejectedly***[4].〕

Qin Zhongyi Now, young man, don't you think it's about time we raised the rent a bit? The **pittance**[5] your father used to pay me as rent won't even keep me in tea!

Wang Lifa Of course, sir, how rig you are! But there's no need for you to bother yourself over such small matters. Send your **steward**[6] round, I'll work it out with him. I'll certainly pay what's fair. Yes I will, sir!

Qin Zhongyi You **rogue**[7], you're even more crafty than your father. You just wait, one of these days I'll take this place back.

Wang Lifa You're joking, sir! I know perfectly well you're concerned about my welfare. You'd never drive me out on to the streets, to sell tea from an earthenware pot!

Qin Zhongyi Just you wait!

〔*The Peasant Woman enters, leading in her hand the Little Girl, with a* ***straw***[8] *stuck in her hair, indicating that she is for sale. Li San is on*

她们俩慢慢地往里走。茶客们忽然都停止说笑，看着她们。

Notes

① twinge /twindʒ/ *n.* (生理，心理上的)剧痛，刺痛

② banter /'bæntə/ *n.* 戏谑，嘲弄

小　妞　（走到屋子中间，立住）妈，我饿！我饿！

〔乡妇呆视着小妞，忽然腿一软，坐在地上，掩面低泣。

③ sob /sɔb/ *v.* 哭诉，哭泣

秦仲义　（对王利发）轰出去！

王利发　是！出去吧，这里坐不住！

乡　妇　哪位行行好？要这个孩子，二两银子！

常四爷　李三，要两个烂肉面，带她们到门外吃去！

④ fetch /fetʃ/ *v.* 接来，取来

李　三　是啦！（过去对乡妇）起来，门口等着去，我给你们端面来！

乡　妇　（立起，抹泪往外走，好像忘了孩子；走了两步，又转回身来，搂住小妞吻她）宝贝！宝贝！

⑤ dazed /deizd/ *a.* 茫然的

王利发　快着点吧！

〔乡妇、小妞走出去。李三随后端出两碗面去。

the point of stopping them, but, feeling a **twinge**[①] *of pity, leaves them alone. The two make their way slowly into the teahouse. The customers suddenly stop their talk and* **banter**[②] *and watch them.*〕

Little girl 〔*stopping in the middle of the room*〕Ma! I'm hungry! I'm hungry!

〔*The Peasant Woman looks blankly at the Little Girl. Suddenly her legs give way, she sinks to the floor and* **sobs**[③] *into her hands.*〕

Qin Zhongyi 〔*to Wang Lifa*〕Get rid of them!

Wang Lifa Yes, sir. Go away! You can't stay here.

Peasant woman Won't some kind person do a good deed? Take this child! Only two taels of silver!

Chang Li San, **fetch**[④] two bowls of noodles, and take them outside to eat.

Li San Yes, sir! 〔*Going over to the Peasant Woman*〕Get up! Wait at the entrance. I'll get you the noodles.

Peasant woman 〔*rises and goes to the entrance wiping her tears, looking* **dazed**[⑤] *as if she has forgotten about the child. After a few steps, she suddenly turns around, takes the child in her arms, kissing her*〕Pet! Pet!

Wang Lifa Now, now, move on!

〔*The Peasant Woman and the Little Girl go out. Li San follows them a moment later with two*

王利发 （过来）常四爷，您是积德行好，赏给她们面吃！可是，我告诉您：这路事儿太多了，太多了！谁也管不了！（对秦仲义）二爷，您看我说的对不对？

常四爷 （对松二爷）二爷，我看哪，大清国要完！

秦仲义 （老气横秋地）完不完，并不在乎有人给穷人们一碗面吃没有。小王，说真的，我真想收回这里的房子！

王利发 您别那么办哪，二爷！

秦仲义 我不但收回房子，而且把乡下的地，城里的买卖也都卖了！

王利发 那为什么呢？

秦仲义 把本钱拢在一块儿，开工厂！

王利发 开工厂？

秦仲义 嗯，顶大顶大的工厂！那才救得了穷人，那才能抵制外货，那才能救国！（对王利发说而眼看着常四爷）唉，我跟你说这些干什么，你不懂！

王利发 您就专为别人，把财产都出手，不顾自己了吗？

Notes

① softhearted *a.* 心地好的，和蔼的

② empire /'empaiə/ *n.* 帝国

③ capital /'kæpitəl/ *n.* 资产

④ get rid of 摆脱，除去

⑤ property /'prɔpəti/ *n.* 财产

⑥ for the sake of 为了……的利益

bowls of noodles.〕

Wang Lifa 〔*coming over*〕 Master Chang, you're really **softhearted**① giving them noodles! But let me tell you, there are so many cases like this. Too many! You can't help them all. 〔*To Qin Zhongyi*〕 Don't you think I'm rig, sir?

Chang 〔*to Song*〕 It seems to me, the Great Qing **Empire**② is done for!

Qin Zhongyi 〔*imperiously*〕 Whether it's done for or not doesn't depend on giving bowls of noodles to the poor! Really, Wang, I'm serious about taking back this house.

Wang Lifa But you can't do that, sir!

Qin Zhongyi Oh, yes, I can. Not only the houses, but also the shops in the city and the land in the countryside.I'm going to sell them all!

Wang Lifa But why?

Qin Zhongyi I'm going to put all my **capital**③ together and start a factory!

Wang Lifa A factory!

Qin Zhongyi Exactly. A big... really big factory! That's the only way to help the poor, keep out foreign goods and save the empire. 〔*Speaking to Wang Lifa but with his eyes on Chang*〕 But what's the use of talking to you about such things? It's above your head.

Wang Lifa Do you mean you're going to **get rid of**④ all your **property**⑤, just **for the sake of**⑥ others, with no thoug for yourself?

秦仲义 你不懂！只有那么办，国家才能富强！好啦，我该走啦。我亲眼看见了，你的生意不错，你甭再要无赖，不长房钱！

王利发 您等等，我给您叫车去！

秦仲义 用不着，我愿意蹓跶蹓跶！

〔秦仲义往外走，王利发送。

〔小牛儿搀着庞太监走进来。小牛儿提着水烟袋。

庞太监 哟！秦二爷！

秦仲义 庞老爷！这两天您心里安顿了吧？

庞太监 那还用说吗？天下太平了：圣旨下来，谭嗣同问斩！告诉您，谁敢改祖宗的章程，谁就掉脑袋！

秦仲义 我早就知道！

〔茶客们忽然全静寂起来，几乎是闭住呼吸地听着。

庞太监 您聪明，二爷，要不然您怎么发财呢！

秦仲义 我那点财产，不值一提！

庞太监 太客气了吧？您看，全北京城谁不知道秦二爷！您比做官的还厉害呢！听说

Notes

① prosperous /ˈprɔspərəs/ *a.* 繁荣的，兴旺的

② trick /trik/ *n.* 诡计，欺诈

③ pipe /paip/ *n.* 管，烟斗

④ edict /ˈiːdikt/ *n.* 布告

⑤ proclaim /prəˈkleim/ *v.* 宣布，公告

⑥ be sentenced to death 判处死刑

⑦ meddle with 干涉，瞎管

⑧ statute /ˈstætjuːt/ *n.* 法令，法规

⑨ chop off 砍掉

⑩ hold one's breath 屏息

⑪ mint /mint/ *n.* 巨额

Qin Zhongyi You wouldn't understand. It's the only way to make the country **prosperous**[1] and strong. All rig, time for me to go. Now, I've seen with my own eyes that you're doing good business. Don't you dare play your **tricks**[2] and refuse to raise the rent!

Wang Lifa Just a moment. I'll get you a cart!

Qin Zhongyi Don't bother. I'd rather walk.

〔*Qin Zhongyi turns to go with Wang Lifa seeing him off.*〕

〔*Eunuch Pang enters, supported by Xiao Niur who is carrying a water* ***pipe***[3].〕

Eunuch Pang Why, Master Qin!

Qin Zhongyi Your Excellency, Master Pang! You must be feeling a lot more relaxed these past few days.

Eunuch Pang Of course. Peace reigns once more. The Imperial **Edict**[4] has been **proclaimed**[5] and Tan Sitong **is sentenced to death**[6]. I tell you, anyone who dares to **meddle with**[7] the **statutes**[8] laid down by our ancestors will have his bean **chopped off**[9]!

Qin Zhongyi I always knew that.

〔*The customers are suddenly silent, as if* ***holding their breath***[10] *listening.*〕

Eunuch Pang Ah, yes, you're so smart! That's why you've made such a **mint**[11].

Qin Zhongyi My little bit of property isn't worth mentioning.

Eunuch Pang How modest you are! Who in Beijing hasn't heard of Master Qin? You're more powerful than the

呀，好些财主都讲维新！

秦仲义 不能这么说，我那点威风在您的面前可就施展不出来了！哈哈哈！

庞太监 说得好，咱们就八仙过海，各显其能吧！哈哈哈！

秦仲义 改天过去给您请安，再见！（下）

庞太监 （自言自语）哼，凭这么个小财主也敢跟我逗嘴皮子，年头真是改了！（问王利发）刘麻子在这儿哪？

王利发 总管，您里边歇着吧！

〔刘麻子早已看见庞太监，但不敢靠近，怕打搅了庞太监、秦仲义的谈话。

刘麻子 喝，我的老爷子！您吉祥！我等了您好大半天了！（搀庞太监往里面走）

〔宋恩子、吴祥子过来请安，庞太监对他们耳语。

〔众茶客静默了一阵之后，开始议论纷纷。

茶客甲 谭嗣同是谁？

茶客乙 好像听说过！反正犯了大罪，要不，怎

Notes

① mandarin /'mændərin/ *n.* 满清官吏

② wield /wiːld/ *v.* 使用，挥舞

③ mutter /'mʌtə/ *v.* 喃喃自语，出怨言

④ upstart /'ʌpstɑːt/ *n.* 暴富者，暴发户

⑤ bandy /'bændi/ *v.* 把……打来打去，往复投掷

⑥ refrain /ri'frein/ *v.* 节制，避免

⑦ bestow /bi'stəu/ *v.* 授予，赐予

⑧ resume /ri'zjuːm/ *v.* 再继续，重新开始

mandarins[1]. I've heard it whispered that quite a number of the rich support the Reformists.

Qin Zhongyi Well, I wouldn't say that. What little influence I may **wield**[2] won't go far in your presence. Ha! Ha! Ha!

Eunuch Pang Well said! Let's both try our best, and see what happens. Ha! Ha! Ha!

Qin Zhongyi Allow me the pleasure of paying you a visit one of these days. Goodbye! 〔*Exit.*〕

Eunuch Pang 〔***muttering***[3] *to himself*〕 Bah! If an **upstart**[4] like that dares to **bandy**[5] words with me, times must really have changed! 〔*To Wang Lifa*〕 Is Pock-mark Liu here?

Wang Lifa Your Excellency, please take a seat.

〔*Pock-mark Liu had spotted the Eunuch the moment he entered but* ***refrained***[6] *from interrupting the latter's conversation with Qin.*〕

Pock-markliu Oh, my master! May Heaven **bestow**[7] fortune on you! I've been waiting for you for a long time! 〔*Helps Eunuch Pang to sit down.*〕

〔*Song Enz and Wu Xiangz come over to pay their respects. The Eunuch whispers something to them.*〕

〔*The other customers in the teahouse, after being silent for a while,* ***resume***[8] *their conversation.*〕

First customer Who is this Tan Sitong?

Second customer I seem to have heard of him somewhere before.

么会问斩呀!

茶客丙 这两三个月了，有些做官的，念书的，乱折腾乱闹，咱们怎能知道他们捣的什么鬼呀!

茶客丁 得! 不管怎么说，我的铁杆庄稼又保住了! 姓谭的，还有那个康有为，不是说叫旗兵不关钱粮，去自谋生计吗? 心眼儿多毒!

茶客丙 一份钱粮倒叫上头克扣去一大半，咱们也不好过!

茶客丁 那总比没有强啊! 好死不如赖活着，叫我去自己谋生，非死不可!

王利发 诸位主顾，咱们还是莫谈国事吧!

〔大家安静下来，都又各谈各的事。

庞太监 (已坐下) 怎么说? 一个乡下丫头，要二百银子?

刘麻子 (侍立) 乡下人，可长得俊呀! 带进城来，好好地一打扮、调教，准保是又好看，又有规矩! 我给您办事，比给我亲爸爸做事都更尽心，一丝一毫不能

Notes

① commit /kəˈmit/ *v.* 犯罪

② stir up 激起，唤起

③ mischief /ˈmistʃif/ *n.* 灾祸，恶作剧

④ bannerman *n.* 旗人

⑤ subsidy /ˈsʌbsidi/ *n.* 补助金，津贴

⑥ abolish /əˈbɔliʃ/ *v.* 废止，革除

⑦ cream off 取走（某数额的金钱）

⑧ leave off 停止，中断

⑨ peach /piːtʃ/ *n.* ［俚］漂亮的女子

He must have **committed**① a horrible crime. Otherwise he wouldn't be sentenced to death.

Third customer In the past two or three months, some officials and scholars were trying to **stir up**② all sorts of trouble. We'll never know what **mischief**③ they were up to.

Fourth customer One thing's certain. My **Bannerman's**④ **subsidy**⑤ is safe again. That Tan and Kang Youwei were saying all subsidies should be **abolished**⑥ and we should make our own living. I call that wicked!

Third customer Anyway, by the time we get our subsidies, our superiors have **creamed off**⑦ the best part of them. It's a dog's life whichever way you look at it.

Fourth customer Still that's better than nothing! A dog's life's better than no life. If I were to earn my own living, I'd surely starve.

Wang Lifa Gentlemen, let's **leave off**⑧ discussing affairs of state, shall we?

〔*People quieten down and turn to discussing their own affairs once more.*〕

Eunuch Pang 〔*already seated*〕 What's that? Two hundred taels of silver for a country girl!

Pock-markliu 〔*standing in attendance*〕 A country girl, true, but what a **peach**⑨! Once in the city, with a bit of make-up and instruction, you'll have a well-mannered beauty on your hands. I've done

马虎!

〔唐铁嘴又回来了。

王利发 铁嘴，怎么又回来了?

唐铁嘴 街上兵荒马乱的，不知道是怎么回事!

庞太监 还能不搜查搜查谭嗣同的余党吗?唐铁嘴，你放心，没人抓你!

唐铁嘴 嗻，总管，您要能赏给我几个烟泡儿，我可就更有出息了!

〔有几个茶客好像预感到什么灾祸，一个个往外溜。

松二爷 咱们也该走啦!天不早啦!

常四爷 嗻!走吧!

〔二灰衣人——宋恩子和吴祥子走过来。

宋恩子 等等!

常四爷 怎么啦?

宋恩子 刚才你说“大清国要完”?

常四爷 我，我爱大清国，怕它完了!

吴祥子 (对松二爷)你听见了?他是这么说的吗?

松二爷 哥儿们，我们天天在这儿喝茶。王掌

Notes

① leave no stone unturned 千方百计，想尽办法

② be crawling with 挤满，充满

③ nose out 侦察到，打探到

④ oblige /ə'blaidʒ/ *v.* 赐，施恩惠

⑤ stealthily /'stelθili/ *ad.* 暗地里，悄悄地

⑥ law-abiding /ə'baidiŋ/ *a.* 守法的

more than I would for my own father. I **left no stone unturned**[1] trying to serve Your Excellency!

〔*Tang the Oracle comes back.*〕

Wang Lifa Hey, Oracle, what are you doing here again?

Tang the oracle The streets **are crawling with**[2] soldiers and horsemen. What's happening?

Eunuch Pang They have to **nose out**[3] Tan Sitong's supporters, don't they? Don't worry, Oracle, no one wants to lay hands on you.

Tang the oracle Thank you, Your Excellency! Now, if you would **oblige**[4] me with a few grains of your prepared opium, I'd be most grateful.

〔*Several customers sensing trouble, one by one begin to leave* ***stealthily***[5].〕

Song We'd better start moving too. It's getting late.

Chang Rig. Let's go.

〔*The two men in grey gowns — Song Enz and Wu Xiangz approach them.*〕

Song Enz Just a moment!

Chang What's the matter?

Song Enz You said just now, "The Great Qing Empire is done for!" didn't you?

Chang Me? I love the empire! I hope it isn't done for.

Wu Xiangz 〔*to Song*〕You heard him? Did he put it like that?

Song Now, now, gentlemen, we have tea here every day. The manager knows us well. We're both **law-abiding**[6] men.

柜知道：我们都是地道老好人！

吴祥子 问你听见了没有？

松二爷 那，有话好说，二位请坐！

宋恩子 你不说，连你也锁了走！他说“大清国要完”，就是跟谭嗣同一党！

松二爷 我，我听见了，他是说……

宋恩子 （对常四爷）走！

常四爷 上哪儿！事情要交代明白了啊！

宋恩子 你还想拒捕吗？我这儿可带着“王法”呢！（掏出腰中带着的铁链子）

常四爷 告诉你们，我可是旗人！

吴祥子 旗人当汉奸，罪加一等！锁上他！

常四爷 甭锁，我跑不了！

宋恩子 量你也跑不了！（对松二爷）你也走一趟，到堂上实话实说，没你的事！

〔黄胖子同三五个人由后院过来。

黄胖子 得啦，一天云雾散，算我没白跑腿！

松二爷 黄爷！黄爷！

黄胖子 （揉揉眼）谁呀？

松二爷 我！松二！您过来，给说句好话！

黄胖子 （看清）哟，宋爷，吴爷，二位爷办案

Notes

① traitor /'treitə/ *n.* 叛徒，卖国贼

② smooth over 缓和，减轻

③ rub /rʌb/ *v.* 擦，搓，摩擦

Wu Xiangz I'm asking you whether or not you heard him!

Song We can easily settle this. Please take a seat.

Song Enz You refuse to answer? We'll take you in too. Since he said "The Great Qing Empire is done for! " he must be a follower of Tan Sitong.

Song Well, I I heard him, but he was only saying...

Song Enz 〔*to Chang*〕 Get going!

Chang Where to? I demand an explanation!

Song Enz Oho! So you're resisting arrest? Look, I've got the "law" here with me! 〔*Pulls out the iron chain from under his gown.*〕

Chang Remember, I'm a Bannerman!

Wu Xiangz A Bannerman turned **traitor** ① gets a heavier sentence! Chain him!

Chang Don't bother! I won't run away!

Song Enz Just you try! 〔*To Song*〕 You come along too. Tell the truth in court and you won't get into trouble.

〔*Tubby Huang, accompanied by three or four others, comes out from the inner courtyard.*〕

Tubby Huang Well, we've done it again! All been **smoothed over**②! I never come here for nothing!

Song Master Huang! Master Huang!

Tubby Huang 〔***rubbing***③ *his eyes*〕 Who's that?

Song Me! Song! Please come over and put in a good word for us.

Tubby Huang 〔*finally understands the situation, turning to the two*

哪？请吧！

松二爷　黄爷，帮帮忙，给美言两句！

黄胖子　官厅儿管不了的事，我管！官厅儿能管的呀，我不便多嘴！（问大家）是不是？

众　嘛！对！

〔宋恩子、吴祥子带着常四爷、松二爷往外走。

松二爷　（对王利发）看着点我们的鸟笼子！

王利发　您放心，我给送到家里去！

〔常四爷、松二爷、宋恩子、吴祥子同下。

黄胖子　（唐铁嘴告以庞太监在此）哟，老爷在这儿哪？听说要安份儿家，我先给您道喜！

庞太监　等吃喜酒吧！

黄胖子　您赏脸！您赏脸！（下）

〔乡妇端着空碗进来，往柜上放。小妞跟进来。

小　妞　妈！我还饿！

王利发　唉！出去吧！

乡　妇　走吧，乖！

Notes

① escort /is'kɔːt/ *v.* 护卫，护送

② exeunt /'eksiʌnt/ *v.* 退场

secret agents〕So! It's you two gentlemen! On official business, are you? Carry on! Carry on!

Song But Master Huang, please help us. Just a few kind words!

Tubby Huang What the authorities can't handle, I do. But when they can, I keep my nose out! 〔*To all present*〕 Ain't that so?

Customers Yes! That's rig!

〔*Song Enz and Wu Xiangz* **escort** ① *Song and Chang towards the entrance.*〕

Song 〔*to Wang Lifa*〕Please take care of our birds!

Wang Lifa Don't worry, I'll send them to your houses.

〔***Exeunt*** ② *Chang, Song, Song Enz and Wu Xiangz.*〕

Tubby Huang 〔*told by Tang the Oracle that Eunuch Pang is present*〕Ah, Your Excellency! I hear that you are starting a family. Allow me to congratulate you before the happy event.

Eunuch Pang You'll be invited to the banquet!

Tubby Huang What an honour! I'm so honoured! 〔*Exit.*〕

〔*The Peasant Woman enters with the empty bowls, which she puts on the counter. The Little Girl follows her in.*〕

Little girl Ma! I'm still hungry!

Wang Lifa You'd better go now.

Peasant woman Let's go, child.

小　妞	不卖妞妞啦？妈！不卖啦？妈！
乡　妇	乖！（哭着，携小妞下）
	〔康六带着康顺子进来，立在柜台前。
康　六	姑娘！顺子！爸爸不是人，是畜生！可你叫我怎办呢？你不找个吃饭的地方，你饿死！我不弄到手几两银子，就得叫东家活活地打死！你呀，顺子，认命吧，积德吧！
康顺子	我，我……（说不出话来）
刘麻子	（跑过来）你们回来啦？点头啦？好！来见见总管！给总管磕头！
康顺子	我……（要晕倒）
康　六	（扶住女儿）顺子！顺子！
刘麻子	怎么啦？
康　六	又饿又气，昏过去了！顺子！顺子！
庞太监	我要活的，可不要死的！
	〔静场。
茶客甲	（正与茶客乙下象棋）将！你完啦！

——幕　落——

Notes

① faint /feint/ *v.* 昏倒

② upset /ʌp'set/ *a.* 烦乱的，不高兴

③ check /tʃek/ *v.* ［象棋］将军

Little girl You're not going to sell me now? Oh, ma! I won't be sold!

Peasant woman Love! 〔*Weeping, she leads the Little Girl away.*〕

〔*Kang Liu enters leading Kang Shunz. They stand in front of the counter.*〕

Kang Liu My dauger! Oh, Shunz! Your father's a beast! But what can I do? You have to find somewhere to feed yourself or you'll starve. I must get a few taels of silver or our landlord will beat me to death. Shunz, accept your fate and have pity on us!

Kang Shunz I — I — 〔*Unable to speak.*〕

Pock-markliu 〔*rushing over*〕So you're back! She agreed? Good! Come and meet His Excellency. Kneel down before His Excellency!

Kang Shunz I... 〔***Faints***①.〕

Kang Liu 〔*supporting his dauger*〕Shunz! Shunz!

Pock-markliu What's wrong with her?

Kang Liu She's so hungry and **upset**②, she's fainted. Shunz! Shunz!

Eunuch Pang I ordered something alive. I won't take it dead!

〔*Silence.*〕

First customer 〔*playing a chess game with the Second Customer*〕 **Check**③! You're finished!

——CURTAIN——

第二幕

时　间　与前幕相隔十余年，现在是袁世凯死后，帝国主义指使中国军阀进行割据，时时发动内战的时候。初夏，上午。

地　点　同前幕。

〔幕启：北京城内的大茶馆已先后相继关了门。“裕泰”是硕果仅存的一家了，可是为避免被淘汰，它已改变了样子与作风。现在，它的前部仍然卖茶，后部却改成了公寓。前部只卖茶和瓜子什么的；“烂肉面”等等已成为历史名词。厨房挪到后边去，专包公寓住客的伙食。茶座也大加改良：一律是小桌与藤椅，桌上铺着浅绿桌布。墙上的“醉八仙”大画，连财神龛，均已撤去，代以时装美人——外国香烟公司的广告画。“莫谈国事”的纸条可是保存了下来，而且字写的更大。王利发真像个“圣之时者也”，不但没使“裕泰”灭亡，而且使它有

Notes

① instigation /ˌinstiˈgeiʃən/ *n.* 鼓动，煽动
② imperialist /imˈpiəriəlist/ *n.* 帝国主义者
③ regime /reiˈʒiːm/ *n.* 政体，政权
④ rear /riə/ *n.* 后面，背后
⑤ convert /kənˈvəːt/ *v.* 使转变，改造
⑥ refreshment /riˈfreʃmənt/ *n.* 点心，茶点
⑦ undergo /ˌʌndəˈgəu/ *v.* 遭受，经历
⑧ wicker /ˈwikə/ *a.* 枝条，柳条
⑨ intoxicated /inˈtɔksikeitid/ *a.* 喝醉的，极其兴奋的
⑩ shrine /ʃrain/ *n.* 圣地，庙

ACT II

Time *Nearly twenty years later. It is now the period after Yuan Shikai's death, when the warlords, at the* ***instigation***[①] *of the* ***imperialist***[②] *powers, set up their separatist* ***regimes***[③] *by force. There were continual civil wars. Early summer. Before noon.*

Placr *Same as in Act One.*

The curtain rises: he large teahouses in Beijing have closed up shop one by one. Yutai, the only one still open, has had to change both its appearance and line of business in order to survive. The front part continues to serve tea, but the ***rear***[④] *section has been* ***converted***[⑤] *into a boarding-house. Only tea and* ***refreshments***[⑥] *like melon seeds are sold; "noodles with minced pork" are a thing of the past. The stove has been moved to the back, for preparing meals for the lodgers. The teahouse has* ***undergone***[⑦] *a great improvement too. The tables are now smaller, with pale green table-cloths and* ***wicker***[⑧] *chairs. The huge painting of "the* ***intoxicated***[⑨] *eig immortals" on the wall and the* ***shrine***[⑩] *of the god of wealth have disappeared. In their place are*

了新的发展。

〔因为修理门面，茶馆停了几天营业，预备明天开张。王淑芬正和李三忙着布置，把桌椅移了又移，摆了又摆，以期尽善尽美。

〔王淑芬梳时行的圆髻，而李三却还带着小辫儿。

〔二三学生由后面来，与他们打招呼，出去。

王淑芬 （看李三的辫子碍事）三爷，咱们的茶馆改了良，你的小辫儿也该剪了吧？

李　三 改良！改良！越改越凉，冰凉！

王淑芬 也不能那么说！三爷你看，听说西直门的德泰，北新桥的广泰，鼓楼前的天

Notes

① poster /ˈpəustə/ *n.* 海报

② manufacturer /ˌmænjuˈfæktʃərə/ *n.* 制造商

③ script /skript/ *n.* 手稿，手迹

④ adjust /əˈdʒʌst/ *v.* 调整，使……适于

⑤ coil /kɔil/ *v.* 盘绕，卷

⑥ bun /bʌn/ *n.* 髻

⑦ pigtail /ˈpigˌteil/ *n.* 辫子

⑧ stipulate /ˈstipjuleit/ *v.* 规定，明定

__posters__[1] of fashionably dressed beauty-queens — advertisements for foreign cigarette __manufacturers__[2]. The "Do not discuss affairs of state" slips, however, have survived, written in an even larger __script__[3]. Like "a sage who follows the fashions", Wang Lifa has not only managed to keep Yutai going, but has also given it a new look.

The teahouse has not been open for the last few days, owing to slig repairs. Now it is getting ready for its formal opening the following day. Wang Shufen and Li San are busy putting the place in order, trying out different positions for the tables and chairs, __adjusting__[4] and re-adjusting them until the desired perfection is achieved.

Wang Shufen has her hair __coiled__[5] up in a round __bun__[6], fashionable at that time. Li San, however, still wears his __pigtail__[7] __stipulated__[8] by the previous Qing Dynasty.

Two or three students come out of the boarding-house, exchange greetings with them, then go off.

Wang Shufen 〔*not happy about Li San's pigtail*〕 Master Li, with our "reformed" teahouse, don't you think it's time you got rid of that pigtail?

Li San Reformed indeed! Soon you'll have nothing more left to reform!

Wang Shufen Don't put it like that. You must have heard, the Detai Teahouse at Xizhimen, the Guangtai Teahouse

泰，这些大茶馆全先后脚儿关了门！只有咱们裕泰还开着，为什么？不是因为拴子的爸爸懂得改良吗？

李　三　哼！皇上没啦，总算大改良吧？可是改来改去，袁世凯还是要做皇上。袁世凯死后，天下大乱，今儿个打炮，明儿个关城，改良？哼！我还留着我的小辫儿，万一把皇上改回来呢！

王淑芬　别顽固啦，三爷！人家给咱们改了民国，咱们还能不随着走吗？你看，咱们这么一收拾，不比以前干净，好看？专招待文明人，不更体面？可是，你要还带着小辫儿，看着多么不顺眼哪！

李　三　太太，你觉得不顺眼，我还不顺心呢！

王淑芬　哟，你不顺心？怎么？

李　三　你还不明白？前面茶馆，后面公寓，全仗着掌柜的跟我两个人，无论怎么说，也忙不过来呀！

王淑芬　前面的事归他，后面的事不是还有我帮助你吗？

Notes

① emperor /'empərə/ *n.* 皇帝

② mess /mes/ *n.* 乱七八糟

③ fire away *v.* 继续开枪

④ stubborn /'stʌbən/ *a.* 顽固的，倔强的

⑤ eyesore /'aisɔː(r)/ *n.* 刺眼的东西

⑥ sore /sɔ/ *a.* 疼痛的，痛心的

⑦ cope /kəup/ *vi.* 对付，妥善处理

at Beixinqiao and the Tiantai Teahouse in front of the Drum Tower have all closed down. Of all the large teahouses, our Yutai is the only one still in business! Why? Because my husband's good at reforms!

Li San Humph! The **emperor's**① gone, isn't that reform enough for you? But, with all that reforming, Yuan Shikai still wanted to be emperor. After he died, what a **mess**②! Guns **firing away**③ today, the city gates closed tomorrow! Reform indeed! I'll keep my pigtail where it is. What if they decide to reform the reform, and bring the emperor back again?

Wang Shufen Don't be so **stubborn**④, Master Li. Since the country's been reformed and a republic set up for us, we'd better conform, hadn't we? Look at our teahouse. With all the re-arranging, doesn't it look more tidy and smart? Now our customers will be fine gentlemen. Won't that be more respectable? But that pigtail of yours, it's an **eyesore**⑤!

Li San It may be an eyesore to you, but I'm **sore**⑥ about other things!

Wang Shufen Why, what are you sore about?

Li San Don't you know? A teahouse here, a boarding-house there. Only the manager and I! We'll never be able to **cope**⑦!

Wang Shufen Leave the teahouse to him. I'll always lend a hand with the boarding-house.

李　三　就算有你帮助，打扫二十来间屋子，侍候二十多人的伙食，还要沏茶灌水，买东西送信，问问你自己，受得了受不了！

王淑芬　三爷，你说的对！可是呀，这兵荒马乱的年月，能有个事儿做也就得念佛！咱们都得忍着点！

李　三　我干不了！天天睡四五个钟头的觉，谁也不是铁打的！

王淑芬　唉！三爷，这年月谁也舒服不了！你等着，大拴子暑假就高小毕业，二拴子也快长起来，他们一有用处，咱们可就清闲点啦。从老王掌柜在世的时候，你就帮助我们，老朋友，老伙计啦！

〔王利发老气横秋地从后面进来。

李　三　老伙计？二十多年了，他们可给我长过工钱？什么都改良，为什么工钱不跟着改良呢？

王利发　哟！你这是什么话呀？咱们的买卖要是越做越好，我能不给你长工钱吗？得了，明天咱们开张，取个吉利，先别吵嘴，就这么办吧！All rig?

李　三　就怎么办啦？不改我的良，我干不下

Notes

① tether /ˈteðə/ *n.* 界限 at the end of one's tether 山穷水尽

② confident /ˈkɔnfidənt/ *a.* 确信的，自信的

③ be keen on 渴望，喜爱

Li San Even with your help it's too much. Twenty-odd rooms to clean and twenty-odd mouths to feed. Plus making tea, fetching hot water, doing the shopping and delivering letters. Well, I ask you, how can one man do all that?

Wang Shufen You're quite rig, Master Li, but these days you can thank your lucky stars if you have a job at all. We all have to be a bit patient.

Li San Well, I'm at the end of my **tether**①! I can't go on. Only four or five hours' sleep every nig. I'm not made of iron!

Wang Shufen You poor man! But none of us has it easy! You wait, Dashuan will finish primary school this summer and his brother is growing up fast. When they can give us a hand, life will be easier. You've been with us since the days of the old manager. You're our old friend, our old partner!

〔*Wang Lifa enters from the rear, looking very* ***confident***②.〕

Li San Old partner? It's more than twenty years now. Did I ever get a raise? Since you're **so keen on**③ reforms, why don't you reform my wages?

Wang Lifa That's no way to talk! If business gets better, of course I'll give you a raise! Enough of that now. We're opening tomorrow. We need all the luck we can get. Let's not argue. Just leave it at that, all right?

Li San Leave it at what? If you don't reform my wages,

去啦!

〔后面叫：李三！李三！

王利发 崔先生叫，你快去！咱们的事，有工夫再细研究!

李　三 哼!

王淑芬 我说，昨天就关了城门，今儿个还说不定关不关，三爷，这里的事交给掌柜的，你去买点菜吧！别的不说，咸菜总得买下点呀!

〔后面又叫：李三！李三！

李　三 对，后边叫，前边催，把我劈成两半儿好不好！（忿忿地往后走）

王利发 拴子的妈，他岁数大了点，你可得……

王淑芬 他抱怨了大半天了！可是抱怨的对！当着他，我不便直说；对你，我可得说实话：咱们得添人!

王利发 添人得给工钱，咱们赚得出来吗？我要是会干别的，可是还开茶馆，我是孙子!

〔远处隐隐有炮声。

王利发 听听，又他妈的开炮了！你闹，闹！明天开得了张才怪！这是怎么说的!

王淑芬 明白人别说糊涂话，开炮是我闹的?

Notes

① pickled /ˈpikld/ *a.* 腌制的

② turnip /ˈtəːnip/ *n.* 大头菜

③ grumpily /ˈgrʌmpili/ *ad.* 性情乖戾地，脾气粗暴地

④ grouse /graus/ *v.* 埋怨

⑤ budge from 让开，挪开

⑥ rumble /ˈrʌmbl/ *n.* 隆隆声，辘辘声

⑦ cannon /ˈkænən/ *n.* 大炮

I'm leaving!

〔*Someone calls from the rear, "Li San! Li San!"*〕

Wang Lifa Mr Cui is calling you, better hurry up. We can talk about this another time.

Li San Huh!

Wang Shufen Yesterday the city gates were closed and perhaps they'll be closed again today. Master Li, let the manager attend to things here. Please go and buy some food. If nothing else, at least some **pickled**① **turnips**②!

〔*More calling from the rear, "Li San! Li San!"*〕

Li San I like that. Ordering me here and calling me there! You mig as well cut me in half! 〔*Goes off* ***grumpily***③ *to the rear.*〕

Wang Lifa Well, old girl, he's getting on. You'd better...

Wang Shufen He's been **grousing**④ all morning. But he has his grounds. I didn't want to say so in front of him, but I tell you frankly, we must get more help!

Wang Lifa More help means more wages! Where's the money to come from? If I were good at something else but refused to **budge from**⑤ this teahouse, then I'd be a bloody fool!

〔*Distant* ***rumbling***⑥ *of* ***cannons***⑦.〕

Wang Lifa Those bloody cannons are at it again! And you stand there making a scene! How are we going to open tomorrow? What a mess!

Wang Shufen I didn't expect to hear such nonsense from you!

王利发　别再瞎扯，干活儿去！嘿！

王淑芬　早晚不是累死，就得叫炮轰死，我看透了！（慢慢地往后边走）

王利发　（温和了些）拴子的妈，甭害怕，开过多少回炮，一回也没打死咱们，北京城是宝地！

王淑芬　心哪，老跳到嗓子眼里，宝地！我给三爷拿菜钱去。（下）

〔一群男女难民在门外央告。

难　民　掌柜的，行行好，可怜可怜吧！

王利发　走吧，我这儿不打发，还没开张！

难　民　可怜可怜吧！我们都是逃难的！

王利发　别耽误工夫！我自己还顾不了自己呢！

〔巡警上。

巡　警　走！滚！快着！

〔难民散去。

王利发　怎样啊？六爷！又打得紧吗？

巡　警　紧！紧得厉害！仗打得不紧，怎能够有这么多难民呢！上面交派下来，你出八十斤大饼，十二点交齐！城里的兵带着

Notes

① reluctantly /ri'lʌktəntli/ *ad.* 不情愿地，嫌恶地

② relent /ri'lent/ *v.* 变宽厚，动怜悯之心

③ jumpy /'dʒʌmpi/ *a.* 跳跃的，神经质的

④ cannonade /kænə'neid/ *n.* 炮击

⑤ refugee /ˌrefju(ː)'dʒiː/ *n.* 难民

⑥ buzz off *v.* 匆忙离去

⑦ disperse /dis'pəːs/ *v.* 分散，散开

What have the cannons got to do with me?

Wang Lifa Oh, stop arguing! Go and do some work!

Wang Shufen One thing's certain. Either your slave-driving or those cannons will finish me! 〔*Goes off to the rear* ***reluctantly***①.〕

Wang Lifa 〔***relenting***②〕 Now, now, old girl, no need to be so **jumpy**③! We've been through these **cannonades**④ quite a few times, but we've never been hit. Beijing's a charmed city!

Wang Shufen Charmed indeed! My heart's always in my mouth! Well, I'll go and get some money for Master Li to do the shopping. 〔*Exit.*〕

〔*A group of* ***refugees***⑤ *gather at the entrance, begging.*〕

Refugees Kind sir! Do a good deed. Take pity on us!

Wang Lifa Move on. We're not handing out anything today. We're not open yet.

Refugees Have mercy! We're all refugees.

Wang Lifa You're wasting your time! I haven't even enough for myself!

〔*The Policeman enters.*〕

Policeman Go away! **Buzz off**⑥! Be quick about it!

〔*The refugees* ***disperse***⑦.〕

Wang Lifa How are things, my friend? Is the figing fierce?

Policeman Very fierce! Otherwise there wouldn't be all these refugees. We've been instructed by our superiors that you're to provide us with eigy catties of

干粮，才能出去打仗啊!

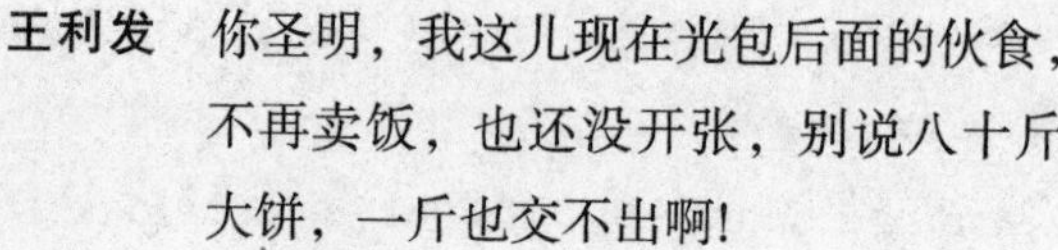

王利发 你圣明，我这儿现在光包后面的伙食，不再卖饭，也还没开张，别说八十斤大饼，一斤也交不出啊!

巡　警 你有你的理由，我有我的命令，你瞧着办吧!（要走）

王利发 您等等! 我这儿千真万确还没开张，这您知道! 开张以后，还得多麻烦您呢! 得啦，您买包茶叶喝吧!（递钞票）您多给美言几句，我感恩不尽!

巡　警 （接票子）我给你说说看，行不行可不保准!

〔三五个大兵，军装破烂，都背着枪，闯进门口。

巡　警 老总们，我这儿正查户口呢，这儿还没开张!

大　兵 屌!

巡　警 王掌柜，孝敬老总们点茶钱，请他们到别处喝去吧!

王利发 老总们，实在对不起，还没开张，要不然，诸位住在这儿，一定欢迎!（递钞票给巡警）

巡　警 （转递给兵们）得啦，老总们多原谅，

Notes

① unleavened /ʌn'levnd/ *a.* 没放酵粉的

② packet /'pækit/ *n.* 小包

③ banknote /'bæŋknəut/ *n.* 纸币

④ count on 依靠，指望

⑤ tattered /'tætəd/ *a.* 破烂的，穿破烂衣的

⑥ rifle /'raifl/ *n.* 步枪

⑦ resident /'rezidənt/ *n.* 居民

⑧ billet /'bilit/ *v.* 给（部队）安排住处

unleavened[1] pancakes before noon. We must feed the soldiers in the city before sending them out to the battlefield, mustn't we?

Wang Lifa That's reasonable! But you know I only provide food for the lodgers now. The teahouse doesn't servemeals any more. And we haven't opened yet. I can't even hand over one catty of pancakes, let alone eigy!

Policeman You have your excuses, I have my orders! Well, do as you like. 〔*Makes as if he is going away.*〕

Wang Lifa Wait a minute! I'm not open yet. You know that! When we are, we'll need your help even more. Take this and buy yourself a small **packet**[2] of tea. 〔*Hands over some* ***banknotes***[3]*.*〕 Put in a good word for me and I'll be most grateful!

Policeman 〔*accepting the money*〕All rig, I'll try, but don't **count on**[4] it.

〔*Three to five soldiers in* ***tattered***[5] *uniforms, all armed with* ***rifles***[6]*, charge in.*〕

Policeman Look here, sirs, I'm making a routine check of the **residents**[7]. This place isn't open yet.

A soldier Balls!

Policeman Manager Wang, offer them some money for tea. Then they'll go elsewhere.

Wang Lifa Sirs, I'm so sorry we're not in business yet, otherwise we'd be honoured to have you **billeted**[8] here. 〔*Hands over some banknotes to the Policeman.*〕

Policeman 〔*passing on the money to the soldiers*〕 I'm sure you'll

他实在没法招待诸位!

大　兵　屌! 谁要钞票? 要现大洋!

王利发　老总们，让我哪儿找现大洋去呢?

大　兵　屌! 凑他个小舅子!

巡　警　快! 再添点!

王利发　(掏) 老总们，我要是还有一块，请把房子烧了! (递钞票)

大　兵　屌! (接钱下，顺手拿走两块新桌布)

巡　警　得，我给你挡住了一场大祸! 他们不走呀，你就全完，连一个茶碗也剩不下!

王利发　我永远忘不了您这点好处!

巡　警　可是为这点功劳，你不得另有份意思吗?

王利发　对! 您圣明，我胡涂! 可是，您搜我吧，真一个铜子儿也没有啦! (掀起褂子，让他搜) 您搜! 您搜!

巡　警　我干不过你! 明天见，明天还不定是风是雨呢! (下)

王利发　您慢走! (看巡警走去，跺脚) 他妈的! 打仗，打仗! 今天打，明天打，老打，打他妈的什么呢?

〔唐铁嘴进来，还是那么瘦，那么脏，可是穿着绸子夹袍。

Notes

① snatch away 夺走

② stamp /stæmp/ *v.* 顿足

③ emaciate /iˈmeiʃieit/ *v.* 使消瘦，使憔悴

understand. He really can't serve you today.

A soldier Balls! Who wants paper money? Give us silver dollars!

Wang Lifa Sirs, where can I get silver dollars?

A soldier Balls! Beat the shit out of him!

Policeman Quick! Give them some more!

Wang Lifa 〔*taking the money out of his pocket*〕 You can burn my house down! I haven't one dollar more! 〔*Hands over paper money.*〕

A soldier Balls. 〔*Takes money, turns to go out, and, in passing,* ***snatches away*** [①] *two new tablecloths. Exeunt the soldiers.*〕

Policeman There! Saved you from real trouble. If they'd stayed, it would have been the end of you! Not a single teacup left!

Wang Lifa And I mustn't forget such a service, eh?

Policeman Aren't you going to do something about it then?

Wang Lifa Rig! How stupid of me! You better search me, I haven't a copper left. 〔*Liftingup his gown to be searched*〕 Go ahead, search me!

Policeman OK, you win. See you tomorrow. Tomorrow's anybody's guess! 〔*Exit.*〕

Wang Lifa Mind your step! 〔***Stamps***[②] *his foot when the Policeman has gone.*〕 Damn it! War, war, all the bloody time! What the hell are you figing about?

〔*Tang the Oracle enters. He is as* ***emaciated***[③] *and as dirty as ever, but now he wears a silk gown.*〕

唐铁嘴　王掌柜！我来给你道喜！

王利发　（还生着气）哟！唐先生？我可不再白送茶喝！（打量，有了笑容）你混的不错呀！穿上绸子啦！

唐铁嘴　比以前好了一点！我感谢这个年月！

王利发　这个年月还值得感谢！听着有点不搭调！

唐铁嘴　年头越乱，我的生意越好！这年月，谁活着谁死都碰运气，怎能不多算算命、相相面呢？你说对不对？

王利发　Yes，也有这么一说！

唐铁嘴　听说后面改了公寓，租给我一间屋子，好不好？

王利发　唐先生，你那点嗜好，在我这儿恐怕……

唐铁嘴　我已经不吃大烟了！

王利发　真的？你可真要发财了！

唐铁嘴　我改抽"白面儿"啦。（指墙上的香烟广告）你看，哈德门烟是又长又松，（掏出烟来表演）一顿就空出一大块，正好放"白面儿"。大英帝国的烟，日本的"白面儿"，两大强国侍候着我一个人，这点福气还小吗？

Notes

① chaos /'keiɔs/ *n.* 混乱

② addiction /ə'dikʃən/ *n.* 耽溺，上瘾

③ heroin /'herəuin/ *n.* 海洛因

Tang the oracle Ah, Manager Wang. Congratulations!

Wang Lifa [*still grumpy*] I t's Mr Tang! No free tea any more. [*Takes another look at him. Smiles.*] So, you're doing all rig. In silk, too!

Tang the oracle Somewhat better off than before, thanks to the times.

Wang Lifa Thanks to the times? Say that again!

Tang the oracle The more **chaos**[1] the better my business. Nowadays life and death are a matter of luck. More andmore people want their fortunes told, their features read. You understand?

Wang Lifa Well, that's one way of looking at it!

Tang the oracle I hear you've converted the courtyard into a boarding-house. What about renting me a room?

Wang Lifa Now, Mr Tang, with that **addiction**[2] of yours, don't you think... ?

Tang the oracle I've given up opium.

Wang Lifa What! Then you'll be able to make something of yourself!

Tang the oracle I've taken up **heroin**[3] instead. [*Pointing at the cigarette advertisement on the wall*] Look, see that "Hatamen" brand of cigarettes. They're long and the tobacco's loosely packed. [*Taking out a cigarette to demonstrate his point*] By knocking one end gently you get an empty space, just rig for heroin. British imperial cigarettes and Japanese heroin! Two great powers looking after poor little

王利发　福气不小！不小！可是，我这儿已经住满了人，什么时候有了空房，我准给你留着！

唐铁嘴　你呀，看不起我，怕我给不了房租！

王利发　没有的事！都是久在街面上混的人，谁能看不起谁呢？这是知心话吧？

唐铁嘴　你的嘴呀比我的还花哨！

王利发　我可不光耍嘴皮子，我的心放得正！这十多年了，你白喝过我多少碗茶？你自己算算！你现在混的不错，你想着还我茶钱没有？

唐铁嘴　赶明儿我一总还给你，那一共才有几个钱呢！（搭讪着往外走）

〔街上卖报的喊叫："长辛店大战的新闻，买报瞧，瞧长辛店大战的新闻！"报童向内探头。

报　童　掌柜的，长辛店大战的新闻，来一张瞧瞧？

王利发　有不打仗的新闻没有？

报　童　也许有，您自己找！

① vacancy /'veikənsi/ *n.* 空白，空缺

② retreat /ri'triːt/ *n.* 撤退

③ poke in 干涉，探听

me. Aren't I lucky?

Wang Lifa Yes, very lucky indeed! But our place is full up. As soon as I get a **vacancy**①, I'll keep it for you.

Tang the oracle I know, you don't think much of me. You're afraid I won't pay the rent.

Wang Lifa Nothing of the sort! We all grew up in the streets. It's not for us to look down on one another. See, I'm being perfectly frank like an old friend!

Tang the oracle You've got a smooth tongue! Better than mine!

Wang Lifa I'm not just talking. My heart's in the rig place. How many cups of free tea have you had off me all these years? Count for yourself. Now that you're better off, has it ever crossed your mind to pay me back?

Tang the oracle I'll pay you back one of these days. But altogether, it won't come to much! 〔*Muttering these words he tries to beat a* ***retreat***②.〕

〔*The Paper Boy crying in the streets, "Read all about the great battle at Changxindian! Paper! Paper! Read all about the great battle at Changxindian!" The Paper Boy* ***pokes his head in***③.〕

Paper boy Hey, manager! Latest news about the figing at Changxindian. Won't you buy a copy?

Wang Lifa Any news about people not figing?

Paper boy Maybe. Look for yourself!

王利发 走！不瞧！

报　童 掌柜的，你不瞧也照样打仗！（对唐铁嘴）先生，您照顾照顾？

唐铁嘴 我不像他，（指王利发）我最关心国事！（拿了一张报，没给钱即走）

〔报童追唐铁嘴下。

王利发 （自言自语）长辛店！长辛店！离这里不远啦！（喊）三爷，三爷！你倒是抓早儿买点菜去呀，待一会儿准关城门，就什么也买不到啦！嘿！（听后面没人应声，含怒往后跑）

〔常四爷提着一串腌萝卜，两只鸡，走进来。

常四爷 王掌柜！

王利发 谁？哟，四爷！您干什么哪？

常四爷 我卖菜呢！自食其力，不含糊！今儿个城外头乱乱哄哄，买不到菜；东抓西抓，抓到这么两只鸡，几斤老腌萝卜。听说你明天开张，也许用的着，特意给你送来了！

Notes

① sneak off 潜出

② knuckle under *v.* 认输，屈服，让步

③ pandemonium /pændi'məʊniəm/ *n.* 混战场，喧哗吵闹

④ come in handy 派上用场

Wang Lifa Go away! I'm not interested!

Paper boy Won't make no difference, manager! The figing'll go on just the same. [*To Tang the Oracle*] Sir, you interested?

Tang the oracle I'm not like him. [*Points at Wang Lifa.*] I'm always concerned about affairs of state. [*Takes a copy and* ***sneaks off*** [1] *without paying.*]

[*The Paper Boy runs off after him.*]

Wang Lifa [*to himself*] Changxindian! Changxindian! That's near here. [*Shouts.*] Master Li! Master Li! You'd better go for the food rig away. The city gates are sure to close soon. We won't be able to get anything. You heard me? [*When no answer comes from the back, he goes towards there angrily.*]

[*Master Chang enters with a string of pickled turnips and two chickens.*]

Chang Manager Wang!

Wang Lifa Who's that? Why, Master Chang! What are you doing these days?

Chang Selling vegetables. Earning my own living. I'm not going to **knuckle under** [2]. Today there was such a **pandemonium** [3] outside the city. I couldn't pick up any vegetables. All I could get were these two chickens and some pickled turnips. I heard you're opening tomorrow. Thoug these mig **come in handy** [4], so I broug them along.

王利发 我谢谢您！我这儿正没有辙呢！

常四爷 （四下里看）好啊！好啊！收拾得好啊！大茶馆全关了，就是你有心路，能随机应变地改良！

王利发 别夸奖我啦！我尽力而为，可就怕天下老这么乱七八糟！

常四爷 像我这样的人算是坐不起这样的茶馆喽！

〔松二爷走进来，穿的很寒酸，可是还提着鸟笼。

松二爷 王掌柜！听说明天开张，我来道喜！（看见常四爷）哎哟！四爷，可想死我喽！

常四爷 二哥！你好哇？

王利发 都坐下吧！

松二爷 王掌柜，你好？太太好？少爷好？生意好？

王利发 （一劲儿说）好！托福！（提起鸡与咸菜）四爷，多少钱？

常四爷 瞧着给，该给多少给多少！

王利发 对！我给你们弄壶茶来！（提物到后面去）

松二爷 四爷，你，你怎么样啊？

常四爷 卖青菜哪！铁杆庄稼没有啦，还不卖膀子力气吗？二爷，您怎么样啊？

Notes

① compliment /ˈkɔmplimənt/ *n.* 称赞，恭维

② posh /pɔʃ/ *a.* 漂亮的，时髦的

③ threadbare /ˈθredbɛə/ *a.* 磨破的，陈腐的

④ missus /ˈmisəz/ *n.* （已婚的）……夫人

⑤ earn one's own living 自力更生，自谋生路

Wang Lifa Thanks a lot! I didn't see how I was going to manage.

Chang [*taking a look around*] Nice! Very nice! You've done it up well! All the large teahouses have closed down. You were the only one sharp enough to make the most of the changes and reforms.

Wang Lifa Thanks for the **compliment**[1]! I do my best, but if the country carries on in this mess, it'll all be wasted.

Chang Well, the likes of me won't be able to afford a seat in such a **posh**[2] teahouse, that's for sure!

[*Master Song enters, his clothes looking* ***threadbare***[3] *but still carrying his bird-cage.*]

Song Manager Wang! You're opening tomorrow? I've come to offer my congratulations! [*Sees Master Chang.*] Oh, my old friend! How I've missed you!

Chang Master Song, my brother! How've you been?

Wang Lifa Why don't you both sit down?

Song Oh, Manager Wang! How are you? How's the **missus**[4]? How are your boys? How's business?

Wang Lifa [*trying to answer all the greetings*] Very well, thank you. [*Picks up the chickens and the pickled turnips.*] Master Chang, what do I owe you?

Chang As you like. Whatever you think's fair.

Wang Lifa Of course! I'll get you a pot of tea. [*Goes to the back with the things.*]

Song Master Chang, how, how's life treated you?

Chang Now I'm selling vegetables! Since the Bannerman's subsidy was abolished, I **earn my own living**[5]. What

松二爷 怎么样？我想大哭一场！看见我这身衣裳没有？我还像个人吗？

常四爷 二哥，你能写能算，难道找不到点事儿做？

松二爷 嗐，谁愿意瞪着眼挨饿呢！可是，谁要咱们旗人呢！想起来呀，大清国不一定好啊，可是到了民国，我挨了饿！

王利发 （端着一壶茶回来。给常四爷钱）不知道您花了多少，我就给这么点吧！

常四爷 （接钱，没看，揣在怀里）没关系！

王利发 二爷，（指鸟笼）还是黄鸟吧？哨的怎样？

松二爷 嗻，还是黄鸟！我饿着，也不能叫鸟儿饿着！（有了点精神）你看看，看看，（打开罩子）多么体面！一看见它呀，我就舍不得死啦！

王利发 松二爷，不准说死！有那么一天，您还会走一步好运！

常四爷 二哥，走！找个地方喝两盅儿去！一醉解千愁！王掌柜，我可就不让你啦，没有那么多的钱！

王利发 我也分不开身，就不陪了！

〔常四爷、松二爷正往外走，宋恩子和

Notes

① disgrace /dis'greis/ *n.* 耻辱，不名誉

② drown /draun/ *v.* 淹死

about you?

Song Me? Just hearing you ask that bring tears to my eyes. Look at my clothes! They're a **disgrace**①!

Chang But you read and write, and do accounts! You can't find a job?

Song Exactly. Who wants to starve? Yet who wants a Bannerman! Looking back, the Great Qing Empire wasn't so good, but now, in the Republic, I'm starving!

Wang Lifa 〔*returning with a pot of tea and giving Master Chang some money*〕 I don't know what you spent. Hope that's enough!

Chang 〔*taking the money without counting*〕 Never mind!

Wang Lifa 〔*pointing at the bird-cage*〕 Still mad on orioles? Does it sing well?

Song Of course it's an oriole! I may starve, but I won't allow my bird to. 〔*Cheering up abit*〕 Look! 〔*Opens cover.*〕 He's such a handsome bird! Whenever I look at him, I don't want to die.

Wang Lifa Master Song, you mustn't talk of dying. One of these days your luck will change!

Chang Come, brother, let's go and have a drink. **Drown**② our sorrows in wine. Manager Wang, I won't invite you. Not enough money, you understand?

Wang Lifa I've got work to do, anyway. Forgive me for not keeping you company.

〔*Just as Chang and Song head for the entrance, Song*

吴祥子进来。他们俩仍穿灰色大衫，但袖口瘦了，而且罩上青布马褂。

松二爷 （看清楚是他们，不由地上前请安）原来是你们二位爷！

〔王利发似乎受了松二爷的感染，也请安，弄得二人愣住了。

宋恩子 这是怎么啦？民国好几年了，怎么还请安？你们不会鞠躬吗？

松二爷 我看见您二位的灰大褂呀，就想起了前清的事儿！不能不请安！

王利发 我也那样！我觉得请安比鞠躬更过瘾！

吴祥子 哈哈哈哈！松二爷，你们的铁杆庄稼不行了，我们的灰色大褂反倒成了铁杆庄稼，哈哈哈！（看见常四爷）这不是常四爷吗？

常四爷 是呀，您的眼力不错！戊戌年我就在这儿说了句"大清国要完"，叫您二位给抓了走，坐了一年多的牢！

宋恩子 您的记性可也不错！混的还好吧？

常四爷 托福！从牢里出来，不久就赶上庚子

Notes

① involuntarily /in'vɔləntərili/ *ad.* 不知不觉地，无心地

② disconcerted /ˌdiskən'səːtid/ *a.* 不安的，惊慌的

③ remark /ri'mɑːk/ *n.* 谈起，述说

④ imprison /im'prizn/ *v.* 使……下狱，拘禁

Enz and Wu Xiangz enter. They are still in grey gowns, but with narrower sleeves because of the new fashion, and with black jackets.〕

Song 〔*recognizing them,* ***involuntarily***[①] *goes down on one knee to pay his respects*〕 Oh, it's you, gentlemen.

〔*Wang Lifa, apparently influenced by Song, also greets them in the same way. The two secret agents are* ***disconcerted***[②].〕

Song Enz What's the matter with you? We've been a republic for several years now. No need to bend the knee. Don't you know how to bow in the new style?

Song Seeing your grey gowns makes me feel it's still the Qing Dynasty. I can't help bending my knee!

Wang Lifa Me too. I feel that bending the knee's more satisfying than bowing.

Wu Xiangz Ha! Ha! Master Song, your Bannerman's subsidy used to be a sure source of income. Well, that's all gone now. But our grey gowns proved a better bet, eh? Ha! Ha! 〔*Seeing Master Chang*〕 It's Master Chang, if I'm not mistaken.

Chang Yes, you have a good memory. In 1898 I made the **remark**[③] here, "The Great Qing Empire is done for!" For that I was arrested by you two, and **imprisoned**[④] for more than a year!

Song Enz Your memory's not bad either. Doing all rig these days?

Chang Yes, thank you. It was 1900 soon after I got out of

年；扶清灭洋；我当了义和团，跟洋人打了几仗！闹来闹去，大清国到底是亡了，该亡！我是旗人，可是我得说公道话！现在，每天起五更弄一挑子青菜，绕到十点来钟就卖光。凭力气挣饭吃，我的身上更有劲了！什么时候洋人敢再动兵，我姓常的还准备跟他们打打呢！我是旗人，旗人也是中国人哪？你二位怎么样？

吴祥子 瞎混呗！有皇上的时候，我们给皇上效力，有袁大总统的时候，我们给袁大总统效力；现而今，宋恩子，该怎么说啦？

宋恩子 谁给饭吃，咱们给谁效力！

常四爷 要是洋人给饭吃呢？

松二爷 四爷，咱们走吧！

吴祥子 告诉你，常四爷，要我们效力的都仗着洋人撑腰！没有洋枪洋炮，怎能够打起仗来呢？

松二爷 您说的对！嗻！四爷，走吧！

常四爷 再见吧，二位，盼着你们快快升官发财！（同松二爷下）

宋恩子 这小子！

王利发 （倒茶）常四爷老是那么又倔又硬，别

Notes

① slogan /'sləugən/ *n.* 标语，口号

② annihilate /ə'naiə'leit/ *v.* 消减，废止

③ deserve /di'zə:v/ *v.* 应受，值得

④ dawn /dɔ:n/ *n.* 破晓

⑤ muddle along 混日子，得过且过

⑥ back /bæk/ *v.* 资助，支持

prison, the year of the Boxers. Their **slogan**[1] was "Support the Qing and **annihilate**[2] the foreigners". I joined them and foug a few battles against the foreign armies. But that didn't help. The Great Qing Empire was done for after all! It **deserved**[3] it! I'm a Bannerman, but I must be fair! Now, I'm up everyday before **dawn**[4], carrying two baskets of vegetables to the city. By ten they're sold. I earn my own living and I'm stronger than ever. If foreigners come here again with their armies, I'm ready to fig them. I'm a Bannerman, but Bannermen are Chinese too! How's life treating you two gentlemen?

Wu Xiangz Oh, **muddling along**[5]! When there was an emperor, we served him. When there was President Yuan Shikai, we served him. Now, Song Enz, how should I put it?

Song Enz Now we serve anyone who puts rice in our bowls.

Chang Even foreigners?

Song Master Chang, let's get going!

Wu Xiangz Understand this, Master Chang. Everyone we serve is **backed**[6] by some foreign power. How can anyone make war without foreign arms and guns?

Song You're so rig! So rig! Master Chang, let's go.

Chang Goodbye, gentlemen. I'm sure you'll soon be rewarded and promoted! 〔*Goes off with Song.*〕

Song Enz Bloody fool!

Wang Lifa 〔*pouring out tea*〕 Master Chang has always been

计较他!(让茶)二位喝碗吧,刚沏好的。

宋恩子　后面住着的都是什么人?

王利发　多半是大学生,还有几位熟人。我有登记簿子,随时报告给"巡警阁子"。我拿来,二位看看?

吴祥子　我们不看簿子,看人!

王利发　您甭看,准保都是靠得住的人!

宋恩子　你为什么爱租学生们呢?学生不是什么老实家伙呀!

王利发　这年月,做官的今天上任,明天撤职,做买卖的今天开市,明天关门,都不可靠!只有学生有钱,能够按月交房租,没钱的就上不了大学啊!您看,是这么一笔账不是?

宋恩子　都叫你咂摸透了!你想的对!现在,连我们也欠饷啊!

吴祥子　是呀,所以非天天拿人不可,好得点津贴!

宋恩子　就仗着有错拿,没错放的,拿住人就有津贴!走吧,到后边看看去!

吴祥子　走!

王利发　二位,二位!您放心,准保没错儿!

Notes

① acquaintance /ə'kweintəns/ *n.* 熟人,相识

② promptly /'prɔmptli/ *ad.* 敏捷地,迅速地

③ vouch /vaʊtʃ/ *v.* 担保

④ partial /'pɑːʃəl/ *a.* 偏袒的,偏爱的

⑤ bonus /'bəunəs/ *n.* 红利,奖金

⑥ nick /nik/ *v.* 逮捕

⑦ at random *ad.* 随便地,任意地

stubborn, won't bow down to anyone! Take no notice of him. 〔*Offering them tea*〕 Have a cup, it's fresh.

Song Enz What sort of people do you have as lodgers?

Wang Lifa Mostly university students, and a couple of old **acquaintances**①. I've got a register. Their names are always **promptly**② reported to the local police-station. Shall I fetch it for you?

Wu Xiangz We don't look at books. We look at people!

Wang Lifa No need for that. I can **vouch**③ for them all.

Song Enz Why are you so **partial**④ to students? They're not generally quiet characters.

Wang Lifa Officials one day and out of office the next. It's the same with tradesmen. In business today and broke tomorrow. Can't rely on anyone! Only students have money to pay the rent each month, because you need money to get into university in the first place. That's how I figure it. What do you think?

Song Enz Got it all worked out! You're quite rig. Nowadays even we aren't always paid on time.

Wu Xiangz So that's why we must make arrests everyday, to get our **bonus**⑤.

Song Enz We **nick**⑥ people **at random**⑦, but they never get out at random. As long as we make arrests, we get our bonus. Come on, let's take a look back there!

Wu Xiangz Yes, let's go!

Wang Lifa Gentlemen, gentlemen! Don't trouble yourselves.

宋恩子 不看，拿不到人，谁给我们津贴呢？

吴祥子 王掌柜不愿意咱们看，王掌柜必会给咱们想办法！咱们得给王掌柜留个面子！对吧？王掌柜！

王利发 我……

宋恩子 我出个不很高明的主意：干脆来个包月，每月一号，按阳历算，你把那点……

吴祥子 那点意思！

宋恩子 对，那点意思送到，你省事，我们也省事！

王利发 那点意思得多少呢？

吴祥子 多年的交情，你看着办！你聪明，还能把那点意思闹成不好意思吗？

李　三 （提着菜筐由后面出来）喝，二位爷！（请安）今儿个又得关城门吧！（没等回答，往外走）

〔二三学生匆匆地回来。

学　生 三爷，先别出去，街上抓伕呢！（往后面走去）

李　三 （还往外走）抓去也好，在哪儿也是当苦力！

〔刘麻子丢了魂似地跑来，和李三碰了

Notes

① nab /næb/ *v.* 逮捕，攫取

② solar /ˈsəulə/ *a.* 太阳的

③ calendar /ˈkæləndə/ *n.* 日历

④ token /ˈtəukən/ *n.* 象征，标志

⑤ in haste *ad.* 急速地

⑥ seize /siːz/ *v.* 抓住，突然抓住

⑦ coolly /ˈkuːli/ *n.* 苦力

Everyone behaves himself properly, I assure you.

Song Enz But if we don't take a look, we can't **nab**[1] anyone. How will we get our bonus?

Wu Xiangz Since the manager's not keen to let us have a look, he must have thoug of another way. Oug to try to help him keep up a front. Rig, Manager Wang?

Wang Lifa I...

Song Enz I've an idea. Not all that brilliant perhaps. Let's do it on a monthly basis. On the first of every month, according to the new **solar**[2] **calendar**[3], you'll hand in a....

Wu Xiangz A **token**[4] of friendship!

Song Enz Rig. You'll hand in a token of friendship. That'll save no end of trouble for both sides.

Wang Lifa How much is this token of friendship worth?

Wu Xiangz As old friends, we'll leave that to you. You're a brig fellow. I'm sure you wouldn't want this token of friendship to seem unfriendly, would you?

Li San 〔*entering with a shopping basket*〕 Oh, gentlemen! 〔*Bends down on one knee.*〕 Are the city gates going to be closed again today? 〔*Heads for the entrance without waiting for an answer.*〕

〔*Two or three students return* ***in haste***[5].〕

A Student Master Li, better stay at home. The army's **seizing**[6] people on the streets for **coolies**[7]. 〔*They continue to the rear.*〕

Li San 〔*not stopping*〕 So what? I'm just a coolie here, aren't I?

〔*Pock-mark Liu, frigened out of his wits, rushes in*

个满怀。

李　三　怎么回事呀？吓掉了魂儿啦！

刘麻子　（喘着）别，别，别出去！我差点叫他们抓了去！

王利发　三爷，等一等吧！

李　三　午饭怎么开呢？

王利发　跟大家说一声，中午咸菜饭，没别的办法！晚上吃那两只鸡！

李　三　好吧！（往回走）

刘麻子　我的妈呀，吓死我啦！

宋恩子　你活着，也不过多买卖几个大姑娘！

刘麻子　有人卖，有人买，我不过在中间帮帮忙，能怪我吗？（把桌上的三个茶杯的茶先后喝净）

吴祥子　我可是告诉你，我们哥儿们从前清起就专办革命党，不大爱管贩卖人口，拐带妇女什么的臭事。可是你要叫我们碰见，我们也不再睁一眼闭一眼！还有，像你这样的人，弄进去，准锁在尿桶上！

刘麻子　二位爷，别那么说呀！我不是也快挨饿了吗？您看，以前，我走八旗老爷们、宫里太监们的门子。这么一革命啊，可苦了我啦！现在，人家总长次长，团

Notes

① collide /kə'laid/ *v.* 碰撞，互撞

② squarely /'skweəli/ *ad.*直截了当地，不含糊的

③ piss /pis/ *n.* 尿，小便

and **collides**[1] **squarely**[2] *with Li San.*〕

Li San What's wrong? You look like death!

Pock-markliu 〔*breathlessly*〕Don't — don't go out! They nearly grabbed me!

Wang Lifa Master Li, better leave it for now.

Li San What about lunch?

Wang Lifa Tell everybody there'll only be pickled turnips and rice for lunch. That's the best we can do. For supper, we'll have those two chickens.

Li San As you like. 〔*Goes off to the boarding-house.*〕

Pock-markliu Oh, lord! Almost scared me to death!

Song Enz So what! You'll only buy and sell a few more girls!

Pock-markliu Well, some wish to sell and some wish to buy. All I do is to lend a helping hand! Don't blame me! 〔*He drinks the three cups of left-over tea on the table oneby one.*〕

Wu Xiangz I'm warning you! Since the time of the empire we've been dealing with revolutionaries. We don't like dirtying our hands with slave-traders and pimps like you! But now if we catch you at it, we won't turn a blind eye any more. When the likes of you get pulled in, you can be sure of this, you'll get chained to the **piss**[3]-pot!

Pock-markliu Now, now, gentlemen, no need to put it like that! These days I'm down-and-out like every one else. In the good old days, I had connections with the Manchu nobles and eunuchs of the court. Since the

长师长，要娶姨太太讲究要唱落子的坤角，戏班里的女名角，一花就三千五千现大洋！我干瞧着，摸不着门！我那点芝麻粒大的生意算得了什么呢？

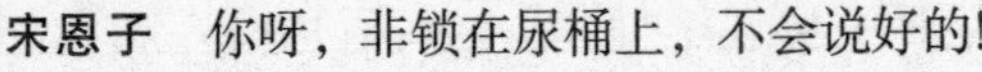

宋恩子 你呀，非锁在尿桶上，不会说好的！

刘麻子 得啦，今天我孝敬不了二位，改天我必有一份儿人心！

吴祥子 你今天就有买卖，要不然，兵荒马乱的，你不会出来！

刘麻子 没有！没有！

宋恩子 你嘴里半句实话也没有！不对我们说真话，没有你的好处！王掌柜，我们出去绕绕；下月一号，按阳历算，别忘了！

王利发 我忘了姓什么，也忘不了您二位这回事！

吴祥子 一言为定啦！（同宋恩子下）

王利发 刘爷，茶喝够了吧？该出去活动活动！

刘麻子 你忙你的，我在这儿等两个朋友。

王利发 咱们可把话说开了，从今以后，你不能再在这儿做你的生意，这儿现在改了良，文明啦！

Notes

① colonel /ˈkəːnl/ *n.* 上校

② concubine /ˈkɔŋkjubain/ *n.* 妾，姨太太

③ pick on 挑选，挑剔

④ tune /tjuːn/ *n.* 声调，语气

⑤ conduct /ˈkɔndʌkt/ *v.* 引导，进行

revolution, I've been leading a dog's life. When ministers and vice-ministers, generals and **colonels**[1] take **concubines**[2], they want sing-song girls and Beijing opera stars. They'll pay thousands of silver dollars for them. I can't even get my toe in the door. Why **pick on**[3] my miserable bit of business?

Song Enz You'll change your **tune**[4] when you're chained to that piss-pot!

Pock-markliu Gentlemen, gentlemen! I've nothing to offer you today, but, one of these days, I promise you something worthwhile.

Wu Xiangz You must be doing a deal of some sort or you wouldn't poke your nose out on a day like this.

Pock-markliu No! I'm not!

Song Enz There's never a word of truth from you. Lying to us won't do you any good! Manager Wang, we'll take a walk around. The first of next month, according to the new solar calendar. Don't forget!

Wang Lifa I may forget my own name, but never your business!

Wu Xiangz That's settled, then! 〔*Goes off with Song Enz.*〕

Wang Lifa Master Liu, had enough tea, I hope? Now take yourself off somewhere else!

Pock-markliu Carry on! Don't mind me! I'm waiting here for a couple of friends.

Wang Lifa I'd better make it clear, once and for all! **Conduct**[5] your line of business elsewhere! We've reformed! We're civilized now!

〔康顺子提着个小包，带着康大力，往里边探头。

康大力 是这里吗？

康顺子 地方对呀，怎么改了样儿？（进来，细看，看见了刘麻子）大力，进来，是这儿！

康大力 找对啦？妈！

康顺子 没错儿！有他在这儿，不会错！

王利发 您找谁？

康顺子 （不语，直奔过刘麻子去）刘麻子，你还认识我吧？（要打，但是伸不出手去，一劲地颤抖）你，你，你个……（要骂，也感到困难）

刘麻子 你这个娘儿们，无缘无故地跟我捣什么乱呢？

康顺子 （挣扎）无缘无故？你，你看看我是谁？一个男子汉，干什么吃不了饭，偏干伤天害理的事！呸！呸！

王利发 这位大嫂，有话好好说！

康顺子 你是掌柜的？你忘了吗？十几年前，有个娶媳妇的太监？

王利发 您，您就是庞太监的那个……

康顺子 都是他（指刘麻子）做的好事，我今天跟他算算账！（又要打，仍未成功）

Notes

① parcel /'pɑːsl/ *n.* 包裹
② peep /piːp/ *v.* 窥视，慢慢露出

③ tremble /'trembl/ *v.* 战悚，忧虑
④ swear /swεə/ *v.* 发誓，咒骂

⑤ decent /'diːsnt/ *a.* 有分寸的，得体的
⑥ filthy /'filθi/ *a.* 污秽的，丑恶的

〔*Kang Shunz, a* **parcel**① *in her hand and leading Kang Dali,* **peeps**② *in at the entrance.*〕

Kang Dali Is this the place?

Kang Shunz It's the place all rig! But it looks so different. 〔*Enters, takes a good look around, and sees Pockmark Liu.*〕Come in, Dali. This is it, alrig!

Kang Dali You sure, ma?

Kang Shunz No mistake! With him here, I'm quite sure.

Wang Lifa Who are you looking for?

Kang Shunz 〔*without ans wering, goes straig to Pock-mark Liu*〕 Pock-mark Liu, recognize me? 〔*Wants to strike him, but is unable to raise her hand. Seized by a fit of* **trembling**③〕 You! You! 〔*Wants to* **swear**④ *at him, but finds it difficult too.*〕

Pock-markliu Why pick on me, missus, for no reason at all!

Kang Shunz 〔*summoning all her strength*〕 No reason? Take a good look at me! Do you see who I am! Couldn't you make a **decent**⑤ living any other way? Do you have to follow your **filthy**⑥ trade? Pah!

Wang Lifa Now, now, madam! Don't get so upset! Calm down!

Kang Shunz Are you the manager? Do you remember, almost twenty years ago, there was a eunuch who boug a wife?

Wang Lifa Ah, so you're Eunuch Pang's...

Kang Shunz 〔*pointing at Pock-mark Liu*〕 And it was all his doing! Today I'm going to make him payfor it! 〔*Attempts*

刘麻子　(躲)你敢！你敢！我好男不跟女斗！(随说随往后退)我，我找人来帮我说说理！(撒腿往后面跑)

王利发　(对康顺子)大嫂，你坐下，有话慢慢说！庞太监呢？

康顺子　(坐下喘气)死啦。叫他的侄子们给饿死的。一改民国呀，他还有钱，可没了势力，所以侄子们敢欺负他。他一死，他的侄子们把我们轰出来了，连一床被子都没给我们！

王利发　这，这是……？

康顺子　我的儿子！

王利发　您的……？

康顺子　也是买来的，给太监当儿子。

康大力　妈！你爸爸当初就在这儿卖了你的？

康顺子　对了，乖！就是这儿，一进这儿的门，我就晕过去了，我永远忘不了这个地方！

康大力　我可不记得我爸爸在哪里卖了我的！

康顺子　那时候，你不是才一岁吗？妈妈把你养大了的，你跟妈妈一条心，对不对？乖！

康大力　那个老东西，掐你，拧你，咬你，还用烟签子扎我！他们人多，咱们打不过他们！要不是你，妈，我准叫他们给打死了！

康顺子　对！他们人多，咱们又太老实！你看，

① out of breath 上气不接下气

② rotter /'rɔtə/ *n.* ［英俚］废物，无赖

③ pinch /pintʃ/ *v.* 掐

④ jab /dʒæb/ *v.* 戳，刺

⑤ skewer /'skjuə/ *n.* 杆，扦状物

to strike him once more, but is still unable to bring herself to do it.〕

Pock-markliu 〔*dodging*〕Lay off! Lay off! What decent man will fig a woman! 〔*Backing away*〕I — I'll get someone to make you see sense. 〔*Runs to the rear.*〕

Wang Lifa 〔*to Kang Shunz*〕Please sit down, madam. Take your time. Where's the Eunuch?

Kang Shunz 〔*sits down,* **out of breath**①〕Dead! Starved to death by his nephews! After the Republic, he still had money, but no more influence. His nephews treated him badly. When he died, they threw us out, without so much as a blanket!

Wang Lifa And this is... ?

Kang Shunz My son.

Wang Lifa Your... ?

Kang Shunz Also boug. As the Eunuch's son.

Kang Dali Ma, is this really where your father sold you?

Kang Shunz That's rig, my dear. This is the place! I fainted as soon as I came in. I'll never forget it.

Kang Dali But I can't remember where my father sold me.

Kang Shunz Well, you were only a year old then. Ma broug you up. We'll always be together, won't we, dear?

Kang Dali That old **rotter**②! He used to **pinch**③ you, bite you and **jab**④ me with his opium **skewer**⑤! There were too many of them. There was nothing we could do. Ma, if it wasn't for you, I'd have died long ago.

Kang Shunz Yes, there were too many of them, and we were

看见刘麻子，我想咬他几口，可是，可是，连一个嘴巴也没打上，我伸不出手去!

康大力 妈，等我长大了，我帮助你打! 我不知道亲妈妈是谁，你就是我的亲妈妈!

康顺子 好! 好! 咱们永远在一块儿，我去挣钱，你去念书! (稍愣了一会儿) 掌柜的，当初我在这儿叫人买了去，咱们总算有缘，你能不能帮帮忙，给我找点事做? 我饿死不要紧，可不能饿死这个无倚无靠的好孩子!

〔王淑芬出来，立在后边听着。

王利发 你会干什么呢?

康顺子 洗洗涮涮、缝缝补补、做家常饭，都会! 我是乡下人，我能吃苦，只要不再做太监的老婆，什么苦处都是甜的!

王利发 要多少钱呢?

康顺子 有三顿饭吃，有个地方睡觉，够大力上学的，就行!

王利发 好吧，我慢慢给你打听着! 你看，十多年前那回事，我到今天还没忘，想起来心里就不痛快!

康顺子 可是，现在我们母子上哪儿去呢?

① slap /slæp/ *v.* 拍击，侮辱

② at a loss 困惑，不知所措

③ sew /sjuː/ *v.* 缝纫，缝合

④ keep an eye open for 严密注视，留心看着

too soft. Just now, when I saw Pock-mark Liu, I wanted to bite him, but I couldn't even **slap**① him. I just couldn't raise my hand!

Kang Dali Ma, when I grow up I'll help you beat them all up! I don't know who my real mother was, so you're my mother, my real mother!

Kang Shunz Yes, my dear. I am! We'll stick together, always! I'll earn some money so you can go to school. 〔***At a loss*** ② *for a moment*〕 Manager, since I was sold here, it seems a bit of luck that we've met again. Can you find me a job of some kind? It's not for myself, but he's a good boy with no one but me to look after him. He mustn't starve.

〔*Wang Shufen enters and stands there unnoticed listening.*〕

Wang Lifa What can you do?

Kang Shunz Washing, **sewing**③, mending, cooking, things like that. I come from the countryside. I don't mind hardwork. As long as I'm not a eunuch's wife, anything will be sweet.

Wang Lifa How much would you want?

Kang Shunz I'll be happy with three meals a day, a bed to sleep in and enough to send Dali to school!

Wang Lifa Rig, I'll **keep an eye open for**④ you. Fact is, I've never forgotten what happened here all these years ago. Always left a bad taste in my mouth!

Kang Shunz But where can we go now?

王利发 回乡下找你的老父亲去!

康顺子 他?他是活是死,我不知道。就是活着,我也不能去找他!他对不起女儿,女儿也不必再叫他爸爸!

王利发 马上就找事,可不大容易!

王淑芬 (过来)她能洗能做,又不多要钱,我留下她了!

王利发 你?

王淑芬 难道我不是内掌柜的?难道我跟李三爷就该累死?

康顺子 掌柜的,试试我!看我不行,您说话,我走!

王淑芬 大嫂,跟我来!

康顺子 当初我是在这儿卖出去的,现在就拿这儿当作娘家吧!大力,来吧!

康大力 掌柜的,你要不打我呀,我会帮助妈妈干活儿!(同王淑芬、康顺子下)

王利发 好家伙,一添就是两张嘴!太监取消了,可把太监的家眷交到这里来了!

李　三 (掩护着刘麻子出来)快走吧!(回去)

王利发 就走吧,还等着真挨两个脆的吗?

刘麻子 我不是说过了吗,等两个朋友?

Notes

① have not a clue 一点不懂

② screen /skriːn/ *v.* 掩蔽,遮蔽

③ snappy /'snæpi/ *a.* 精力充沛的,潇洒的 make it snappy 赶快,干脆一点

Wang Lifa How about going back to the countryside and looking up your old father?

Kang Shunz Him? I **haven't a clue**① if he's alive or dead. Even if he's still around, I won't look him up. He never stood by me, his own dauger, then. I won't call him father now!

Wang Lifa But a job rig away won't be all that easy to find!

Wang Shufen 〔*coming over*〕 She's good at housework and not asking too much. I'll keep her!

Wang Lifa You?

Wang Shufen Don't I run half the teahouse? You want to work me and Master Li to death?

Kang Shunz Manager, give me a chance. Whenever you feel I'm not up to it, just say the word and I'll go.

Wang Shufen Come with me, sister.

Kang Shunz Since I was sold here, this is like my parents' home. Come, Dali.

Kang Dali Manager, if you don't beat me, I'll help with the work, too. 〔*Goes off with Wang Shufen and Kang Shunz.*〕

Wang Lifa Damn! Two more mouths to feed! The Eunuch's gone but I get landed with his family!

Li San 〔*coming out with Pock-mark Liu,* ***screening***② *him*〕 Better get going! 〔*Goes back.*〕

Wang Lifa **Make it snappy**③! Unless you want your face slapped!

Pock-markliu I told you, I have to wait for two friends!

王利发	你呀，叫我说什么才好呢!
刘麻子	有什么法子呢! 隔行如隔山，你老得开茶馆，我老得干我这一行! 到什么时候，我也得干我这一行!

〔老林和老陈满面笑容地走进来。

刘麻子	(二人都比他年轻，他却称呼他们哥哥) 林大哥，陈二哥! (看王利发不满意，赶紧说) 王掌柜，这儿现在没有人，我借个光，下不为例!
王利发	她 (指后边) 可是还在这儿呢!
刘麻子	不要紧了，她不会打人! 就是真打，他们二位也会帮助我!
王利发	你呀! 哼! (到后边去)
刘麻子	坐下吧，谈谈!
老　林	你说吧! 老二!
老　陈	你说吧! 哥!
刘麻子	谁说不一样啊!
老　陈	你说吧，你是大哥!
老　林	那个，你看，我们俩是把兄弟!
老　陈	对! 把兄弟，两个人穿一条裤子的交情!
老　林	他有几块现大洋!
刘麻子	现大洋?
老　陈	林大哥也有几块现大洋!
刘麻子	一共多少块呢? 说个数目!

Notes

① beaming /'biːmiŋ/ *a.* 笑吟吟的

② deserter /di'zəːtə/ *n.* 背弃者，逃亡者

③ address /ə'dres/ *v.* 用特殊的头衔称呼

④ retire /ri'taiə/ *v.* 退下; 离开

Wang Lifa I can't think of a good enough name for you!

Pock-markliu Nothing you can do about it. Once in a trade, always in the trade. You'll always be selling your tea. I'll always be doing my business! Till my dying day!

〔*Lao Lin and Lao Chen enter,* ***beaming***①*.*〕

Pock-markliu 〔*despite the fact that the two* ***deserters***② *are both younger, he insists on* ***addressing*** ③ *them respectfully*〕 Elder Brother Lin! Elder Brother Chen! 〔*Feeling Wang Lifa's anger, he hastily adds.*〕 Manager Wang, there's no one around. Let me borrow your place just this once, I promise it's the last time!

Wang Lifa 〔*pointing to the back*〕 Don't forget she's in there!

Pock-markliu Never mind, she can't do much. If she tries, these fellows can help me.

Wang Lifa You! Bah! 〔***Retires***④ *to the back.*〕

Pock-markliu Sit down. Let's talk it over.

Lao Lin You say it, Second Brother.

Lao Chen No, you say it, Elder Brother.

Pock-markliu What's the difference who speaks?

Lao Chen You say it, you're the Elder Brother.

Lao Lin Well, it's like this, we're sworn brothers.

Lao Chen That's rig! Sworn brothers, so close we'd share the same pair of trousers.

Lao Lin He's got a few silver dollars.

Pock-markliu Silver dollars?

Lao Chen Elder Brother here also has some.

Pock-markliu How much altogether? Tell me!

老　林　那，还不能告诉你咧！

老　陈　事儿能办才说咧！

刘麻子　有现大洋，没有办不了的事！

老　林
老　陈　真的？

刘麻子　说假话是孙子！

老　林　那么，你说吧，老二！

老　陈　还是你说，哥！

老　林　你看，我们是两个人吧？

刘麻子　嗯！

老　陈　两个人穿一条裤子的交情吧？

刘麻子　嗯！

老　林　没人耻笑我们的交情吧？

刘麻子　交情嘛，没人耻笑！

老　陈　也没人耻笑三个人的交情吧？

刘麻子　三个人？都是谁？

老　林　还有个娘儿们！

刘麻子　嗯！嗯！嗯！我明白了，可是不好办，我没办过！你看，平常都说小两口儿，哪有小三口儿的呢！

老　林　不好办？

刘麻子　太不好办啦！

老　林　（问老陈）你看呢？

老　陈　还能白拉倒吗？

Notes

① tricky /'triki/ *a.* 不易处理的，需要技巧的

② triple /'tripl/ *n.* 三个一组

③ call off 取消

Lao Lin We're not going to tell you that yet.

Lao Chen Not till we know if it's possible.

Pock-markliu With silver dollars everything's possible!

Lao Lin
Lao Chen Really?

Pock-markliu If I'm lying to you, I'll be damned!

Lao Lin You say it then, Second Brother.

Lao Chen No, no! You say it, Elder Brother.

Lao Lin See here. There are two of us, rig?

Pock-markliu Rig!

Lao Chen Our friendship's so close we can share the same pair of trousers, rig?

Pock-markliu Rig!

Lao Lin No one would laugh at our friendship, would they?

Pock-markliu Friendship is friendship. Who laughs at that?

Lao Chen And no one makes fun of friendship among three people either, do they?

Pock-markliu Three people? Who?

Lao Lin Us and a woman!

Pock-markliu Oh! Oh! Now I get it! But this is going to be **tricky**①. I've never done anything like it before. People usually talk about some nice young couple. But who's ever heard of a nice young **triple**②?

Lao Lin Tricky, eh?

Pock-markliu Very tricky!

Lao Lin 〔*to Lao Chen*〕What do you think?

Lao Chen We're not going to **call it off**③, are we?

老　林　不能拉倒！当了十几年兵，连半个媳妇都娶不上！他妈的！

刘麻子　不能拉倒，咱们再想想！你们到底一共有多少块现大洋？

〔王利发和崔久峰由后面慢慢走来。刘麻子等停止谈话。

王利发　崔先生，昨天秦二爷派人来请您，您怎么不去呢？您这么有学问，上知天文，下知地理，又做过国会议员，可是住在我这里，天天念经；干嘛不出去做点事呢？您这样的好人，应当出去做官！有您这样的清官，我们小民才能过太平日子！

崔久峰　惭愧！惭愧！做过国会议员，那真是造孽呀！革命有什么用呢，不过自误误人而已！唉！现在我只能修持，忏悔！

王利发　您看秦二爷，他又办工厂，又忙着开银号！

崔久峰　办了工厂、银号又怎么样呢？他说实业救国，他救了谁？救了他自己，越来越有钱了！可是他那点事业，哼，外国人伸出一个小指头，就把他推倒在

Notes

① end up with 结束于
② think over 仔细考虑
③ cease /siːs/ *v.* 停止，终了
④ chant /tʃɑːnt/ *v.* 吟唱，颂扬
⑤ grievous /'griːvəs/ *a.* 痛苦的，严重的
⑥ misled /mis'led/ *v.* 带错
⑦ meditation /medi'teiʃən/ *n.* 沉思，冥想
⑧ repentance /ri'pentəns/ *n.* 后悔，悔改

Lao Lin Hell, no! We've been in the army for more than ten years and can't even **end up with**[①] half a wife? Fuck it!

Pock-markliu We won't call it off. Let's **think it over**[②]! How many silver dollars do you have?

〔*Wang Lifa and Cui Jiufeng come out from the rear, walking slowly. Pock-mark Liu and the two deserters* **cease**[③] *talking.*〕

Wang Lifa Mr Cui, why didn't you go when Master Qin sent you an invitation yesterday? You're a learned man. You know all about heaven and earth. You've been a member of parliament. Yet you shut yourself up here **chanting**[④] Buddhist scriptures! Why not do something more useful? A good man like you should go into politics! With worthy men like you in office, we ordinary folk mig enjoy a few days of peace!

Cui Jiufeng You make me feel ashamed! Yes, I was a member of parliament, a **grievous**[⑤] sin. What has the revolution accomplished? We **misled**[⑥] ourselves and others! Now I spend my days in **meditation**[⑦] and **repentance**[⑧]. That's all I can do!

Wang Lifa But look at Master Qin! Running a factory and getting ready to open a bank!

Cui Jiufeng With all his factories and banks, what can he do? He says he's going to save the country by industry and commerce. But who has he saved? Himself! He's richer than ever. And all his industry and

地，再也起不来！

王利发　您别这么说呀！难道咱们就一点盼望也没有了吗？

崔久峰　难说！很难说！你看，今天王大帅打李大帅，明天赵大师又打王大帅。是谁叫他们打的？

王利发　谁？哪个混蛋？

崔久峰　洋人！

王利发　洋人？我不能明白！

崔久峰　慢慢地你就明白了。有那么一天，你我都得做亡国奴！我干过革命，我的话不是随便说的！

王利发　那么，您就不想想主意，卖卖力气，别叫大家做亡国奴？

崔久峰　我年轻的时候，以天下为己任，的确那么想过！现在，我可看透了，中国非亡不可！

王利发　那也得死马当活马治呀！

崔久峰　死马当活马治？那是妄想！死马不能再活，活马可早晚得死！好啦，我到弘济寺去，秦二爷再派人来找我，你就说，我只会念经，不会干别的！（下）

〔宋恩子、吴祥子又回来了。

王利发　二位！有什么消息没有？

〔宋恩子、吴祥子不语，坐在靠近门口的地方，看着刘麻子等。

Notes

① collapse /kə'læps/ *v.* 倒塌，崩溃

② marshal /'mɑːʃəl/ *n.* 陆空军高级将官

③ wage /weidʒ/ *v.* 开始，进行（战争、运动）

④ colony /'kɔləni/ *n.* 殖民地

⑤ corpse /kɔːps/ *n.* 尸体

commerce will **collapse**[1] if the foreigners lift just one little finger. Then he'll never get on his feet again.

Wang Lifa Oh please don't say that! Isn't there any hope for us?

Cui Giufeng Hard to say. Very hard to say. Now **Marshal**[2] Wang **wages**[3] a war on Marshal Li. The next day Marshal Zhao attacks Marshal Wang. Who's behind it all?

Wang Lifa Who? The bastard!

Cui Giufeng The foreigners.

Wang Lifa The foreigners? I don't understand.

Cui Giufeng One day you will, when China is reduced to a **colony**[4] and all of us are slaves! I took part in the revolution. I know what I'm talking about.

Wang Lifa Then why don't you do something? Save us from being slaves.

Cui Giufeng As a young man, I thoug my ideals could save the world. I tried to follow them. Now I've seen through it all. China's finished!

Wang Lifa But we must try to save her!

Cui Giufeng Save her? That's just wishful thinking! A **corpse**[5] can't be broug back to life. Everything dies sooner or later. Well, I'm off to the Hongji Temple. If Master Qin should send for me again, just tell him I'm only interested in chanting Buddhist scriptures. 〔*Exit.*〕

〔*Song Enz and Wu Xiangz enter again.*〕

Wang Lifa Gentlemen! Any news?

〔*The two say nothing and take seats near the entrance, watching Pock-mark Liu and the two deserters.*〕

〔刘麻子不知如何是好，低下头去。

〔老陈、老林也不知如何是好，相视无言。

〔静默了有一分钟。

老　陈　哥，走吧？

老　林　走！

宋恩子　等等！（立起来，挡住路）

老　陈　怎么啦？

吴祥子　（也立起）你说怎么啦？

〔四人呆呆相视一会儿。

宋恩子　乖乖地跟我们走！

老　林　上哪儿？

吴祥子　逃兵，是吧？有些块现大洋，想在北京藏起来，是吧？有钱就藏起来，没钱就当土匪，是吧？

老　陈　你管得着吗？我一个人揍你这样的八个。（要打）

宋恩子　你？可惜你把枪卖了，是吧？没有枪的干不过有枪的，是吧？（拍了拍身上的枪）我一个人揍你这样的八个！

老　林　都是弟兄，何必呢？都是弟兄！

吴祥子　对啦！坐下谈谈吧！你们是要命呢？还是要现大洋？

老　陈　我们那点钱来的不容易！谁发饷，我们给谁打仗，我们打过多少次仗啊！

① nonplus /'nɔn'plʌs/ *v.* 使困惑

② bandit /'bændit/ *n.* 强盗

③ pat /pæt/ *v.* 轻拍，拍

④ lick /lik/ *v.* 舔，鞭打

[*Pock-mark Liu*, **nonplussed**①, *looks at his toes.*]

[*Lao Lin and Lao Chen, also uncomfortable, look at each other.*]

[*Silence for fully a minute.*]

Lao Chen Elder Brother, shall we go?

Lao Lin Yeah!

Song Enz Just a minute! [*Standing up, he blocks the way.*]

Lao Chen What's up?

Wu Xiangz [*also standing up*] You'd better be telling me what's up!

[*The four of them stare at each other for a moment.*]

Song Enz Better come quietly!

Lao Lin Where to?

Wu Xiangz Deserters, rig? Trying to hide in Beijing, with a few silver dollars in your pockets, rig? When the money runs out, become **bandits**②, rig?

Lao Chen None of your bloody business! I can lick eig of your sort with one hand! [*Prepares to fig.*]

Song Enz You? Pity you sold your gun, rig? Bare hands ain't no match for a gun, rig? [***Patting***③ *the gun under his gown*] I can **lick**④ eig of your sort with one finger! Rig?

Lao Lin We're all brothers, aren't we? No need for unpleasantness.

Wu Xiangz That's more like it. Let's sit down and have a little chat. Make your choice. Your silver dollars or your lives!

Lao Chen We went through hell to earn this bit of money! We foug for whoever paid us! Shit! The number of battles we foug!

宋恩子　逃兵的罪过，你们可也不是不知道！

老　林　咱们讲讲吧，谁叫咱们是弟兄呢！

吴祥子　这像句自己人的话！谈谈吧！

王利发　（在门口）诸位，大令过来了！

老　陈
老　林　啊！（惊慌失措，要往里边跑）

宋恩子　别动！君子一言，把现大洋分给我们一半，保你们俩没事！咱们是自己人！

老　陈
老　林　就那么办！自己人！

〔“大令”进来：二捧刀——刀缠红布——背枪者前导，手捧令箭的在中，四持黑红棍者在后。军官在最后押队。

吴祥子　（和宋恩子、老林、老陈一齐立正，从帽中取出证章，叫军官看）报告官长，我们正在这儿盘查一个逃兵。

军　官　就是他吗？（指刘麻子）

吴祥子　（指刘麻子）就是他！

军　官　绑！

刘麻子　（喊）老爷！我不是！不是！

Notes

① get down to business 开始谈正经事

② panic /ˈpænik/ *n.* 恐慌，惊惶

③ split /split/ *v.* 分离，分开

④ edict /ˈiːdikt/ *n.* 布告

⑤ club /klʌb/ *n.* 棍棒

⑥ dominate /ˈdɔmineit/ *v.* 支配，占优势

⑦ credential /kriˈdenʃəl/ *n.* 国书，凭据

⑧ interrogate /inˈterəgeit/ *v.* 质问，审问

Song Enz But you know very well how they treat deserters!

Lao Lin Let's talk it over. After all, we're all brothers.

Wu Xiangz That's the way to talk among friends. Now let's **get down to business**[①]!

Wang Lifa 〔*at the entrance*〕 Hey! The Execution Squad's coming!

Lao Chen
Lao Lin Oh? 〔*In a* ***panic***[②], *they try to run to the back.*〕

Song Enz Stop! Our word of honour: **Split**[③] the silver dollars with us and you'll be safe. We're friends, rig?

Lao Chen
Lao Lin Yeah! Friends!

〔*The Execution Squad enters: two soldiers carrying rifles and broadswords swathed in red cloth in the lead; one bearing the execution* ***edict***[④] *shaped like a huge arrow in the middle; and four soldiers carrying* ***clubs***[⑤] *painted red at one end and black at the other bringing up the rear. The Officer enters last,* ***dominating***[⑥] *the squad.*〕

Wu Xiangz 〔*standing at attention with Song Enz, Lao Lin and Lao Chen in a line, takes out his* ***credentials***[⑦] *from under his cap and shows it to the Officer*〕May I report, sir? We're **interrogating**[⑧] a deserter here.

Officer 〔*pointing at Pock-mark Liu*〕 Him?

Wu Xiangz 〔*pointing at Pock-mark Liu*〕 Yes, him!

Officer Tie him up!

Pock-markliu 〔*screaming*〕 Sir! I'm not! I'm not!

军　官　绑！（同下）

吴祥子　（对宋恩子）到后面抓两个学生！

宋恩子　走！（同往后疾走）

——幕　落——

Officer Tie him up!

〔*Exeunt the Execution Squad and Pock-mark Liu.*〕

Wu Xiangz 〔*to Song Enz*〕 Let's go and pull in those two students.

Song Enz Yes, come on! 〔*The two hastily head for the boarding-house.*〕

—CURTAIN—

第三幕

Notes

时　间　抗日战争胜利后，国民党特务和美国兵在北京横行的时候。秋，清晨。

地　点　同前幕。

〔幕启：现在，裕泰茶馆的样子可不像前幕那么体面了。藤椅已不见，代以小凳与条凳。自房屋至家具都显着暗淡无光。假若有什么突出惹眼的东西，那就是"莫谈国事"的纸条更多，字也更大了。在这些纸条子旁边还贴着"茶钱先付"的新纸条。

〔一清早，还没有下窗板。王利发的儿子王大拴，垂头丧气地独自收拾屋子。

〔王大拴的妻周秀花，领着小女儿王小花，由后面出来。她们一边走一边说话儿。

王小花　妈，晌午给我做点热汤面吧！好多天没

① dignify /'dignifai/ *v.* 增威严，使高贵

② gloomy /'gluːmi/ *a.* 抑沉的，忧闷的

③ in advance 提前，预先

④ shutter /'ʃʌtə/ *n.* 百叶窗，遮门

ACT III

Time *After the defeat of the Japanese in 1945, the period in which US soldiers and KMT secret service agents were running loose in Beijing. An early morning in autumn.*

Placr *he same as the previous act.*

The curtain rises: he Yutai Teahouse is no longer the **dignified**① *establishment of earlier times. The wicker chairs have disappeared, replaced by stools and benches. Everything, from the building to the furniture, looks* **gloomy**②. *If there is anything outstanding which catches the eye, it is the paper slips with "Do not discuss affairs of state" on them. Their number has increased and the characters enlarged. Alongsides these, new paper slips have been added, with "Please pay* **in advance**③*" on them.*

It is early morning, the wooden **shutters**④ *have not yet been taken down from the windows. Wang Dashuan, Wang Lifa's son, in low spirits, is tidying the premises.*

His wife Zhou Xiuhua, leading their young dauger Wang Xiaohua by the hand, enters from the back. They are talking to each other as they enter.

吃过啦！

周秀花 我知道，乖！可谁知道买得着面买不着呢！就是粮食店里可巧有面，谁知道咱们有钱没有呢！唉！

王小花 就盼着两样都有吧！妈！

周秀花 你倒想得好，可哪能那么容易！去吧，小花，在路上留神吉普车！

王大拴 小花，等等！

王小花 干嘛？爸！

王大拴 昨天晚上……

周秀花 我已经嘱咐过她了！她懂事！

王大拴 你大力叔叔的事万不可对别人说呀！说了，咱们全家都得死！明白吧！

王小花 我不说，打死我也不说！有人问我大力叔叔回来过没有，我就说：他走了好几年，一点消息也没有！

〔康顺子由后面走来。她的腰有点弯，但还硬朗。她一边走一边叫王小花。

康顺子 小花！小花！还没走哪？

王小花 康婆婆，干嘛呀？

康顺子 小花，乖！婆婆再看你一眼，（抚弄王小花的头）多体面哪！吃的不足啊，要不然还得更好看呢！

周秀花 大婶，您是要走吧？

康顺子 是呀！我走，好让你们省点嚼谷呀！大力是我拉扯大的，他叫我走，我怎能

① jeep /dʒiːp/ *n.* 吉普车

② din /din/ *v.* 絮絮不休地说，喧闹

③ stroke /strəuk/ *v.* 抚，抚摸

Wang Xiaohua Ma, make me some hot noodle soup for lunch. It's ages since we've had it.

Zhou Xiuhua I know, pet, but who knows if there'll be any flour in the shops today. Even if there is some, we don't know if we can afford it. What a life!

Wang Xiaohua Let's hope there will be both, ma.

Zhou Xiuhua You can hope, but that won't get you far. Off you go now! Be careful of those **jeeps**① on your way!

Wang Dashuan Xiaohua, wait!

Wang Xiaohua What is it, dad?

Wang Dashuan About last nig...

Zhou Xiuhua I've **dinned**② it into her. She's a sensible child.

Wang Dashuan Never tell anybody about your uncle Dali. If you do, we've all had it! Understand?

Wang Xiaohua I won't say a word, even if they kill me. If I'm asked about Uncle Dali, I'll just say he's been gone for many years. No news about him at all!

〔*Kang Shunz enters from the rear. Her back is now sligly bent, but she's still going strong. She is calling out to Xiaohua as she comes in.*〕

Kang Shunz Xiaohua! Xiaohua! You still here?

Wang Xiaohua Granny Kang, what is it?

Kang Shunz My dear, let me have another look at you. 〔***Stroking***③ *Xiaohua's hair*〕 How pretty! But too thin! With more to eat she'd look even better.

Zhou Xiuhua Aunt, have you made up your mind to go?

Kang Shunz Yes, I'll go. Then I won't be a burden to you. I

不走呢？当初，我刚到这里的时候，他还没有小花这么高呢!

王小花 看大力叔叔现在多么壮实，多么大气!

康顺子 是呀，虽然他只在这儿坐了一袋烟的工夫呀，可是叫我年轻了好几岁！我本来什么也没有，一见着他呀，好像忽然间我什么都有啦！我走，跟着他走，受什么累，吃什么苦，也是香甜的！看他那两只大手，那两只大脚，简直是个顶天立地的男子汉!

王小花 婆婆，我也跟您去!

康顺子 小花，你乖乖地去上学，我会回来看你!

王大拴 小花，上学吧，别迟到!

王小花 婆婆，等我下了学您再走!

康顺子 哎！哎！去吧，乖！（王小花下）

王大拴 大婶，我爸爸叫您走吗?

康顺子 他还没打好了主意，我倒怕呀，大力回来的事儿万一叫人家知道了啊，我又忽然这么一走，也许要连累了你们！这年月不是天天抓人吗？我不能做对不起你们的事!

周秀花 大婶，您走您的，谁逃出去谁得活命！喝茶的不是常低声儿说：想要活命得上西山吗?

王大拴 对!

Notes

① leak out 泄漏，走漏

broug Dali up. Now he wants me to go with him. How can I refuse? When we first came here, he wasn't even as big as Xiaohua is now.

Wang Xiaohua Now, he's so strong. He's wonderful!

Kang Shunz He was here only a few minutes, but I really feel years younger. I haven't a thing in the world, but when I see him, I feel I've everything. Yes, I'll go with him. With him, hard work or sufferings will be sweet. You saw his big hands and feet, a real man!

Wang Xiaohua Granny, I want to go with you!

Kang Shunz Xiaohua, you be a good girl and go to school. I'll come back and see you.

Wang Dashuan Xiaohua, go to school now. Don't be late.

Wang Xiaohua Granny, don't go till I've come back from school.

Kang Shunz Yes, yes! Run along now, my dear!

〔*Exit Wang Xiaohua.*〕

Wang Dashuan Aunt, has dad agreed to let you go?

Kang Shunz He hasn't decided yet. What worries me is, if Dali's visit somehow **leaks out** ① and then I suddenly disappear, it may mean trouble for you. People are getting arrested all the time. I don't want to let you down.

Zhou Xiuhua Now, aunt, you just go ahead. You'll have a chance to live if you go away. Customers are always whispering to each other, "If you want a chance to live, go to the Western Hills."

Wang Dashuan That's rig.

康顺子 小花的妈，来吧，咱们再商量商量！我不能专顾自己，叫你们吃亏！老大，你也好好想想！（同周秀花下）

〔丁宝进来。

丁　宝 嗨，掌柜的，我来啦！

王大拴 你是谁？

丁　宝 小丁宝！小刘麻子叫我来的，他说这儿的老掌柜托他请个女招待。

王大拴 姑娘，你看看，这么个破茶馆，能用女招待吗？我们老掌柜呀，穷得乱出主意！

〔王利发　慢慢地走出来，他还硬朗，穿的可很不整齐。

王利发 老大，你怎么老在背后褒贬老人呢？谁穷得乱出主意呀？下板子去！什么时候了，还不开门！

〔王大拴去下窗板。

丁　宝 老掌柜，你硬朗啊？

王利发 嗯！要有炸酱面的话，我还能吃三大碗呢，可惜没有！十几了？姑娘！

丁　宝 十七！

王利发 才十七？

丁　宝 是呀！妈妈是寡妇，带着我过日子。胜

Notes

① dump /dʌmp/ *n.* 垃圾场

② scheme /skiːm/ *n.* 方案，计划

③ gait /geit/ *n.* 步态

④ shabbily /ˈʃæbili/ *ad.* 衣衫褴褛地，不体面地

⑤ run down 说坏话，贬低

⑥ pack away 吃掉很多，胃口大

Kang Shunz Well, Xiuhua, let's talk it over. I mustn't think of myself only and let all of you suffer for it. Dashuan, you'd better think it over too. 〔*Goes off with Zhou Xiuhua.*〕

Ding Bao Hi, manager, I'm here!

Wang Dashuan Who're you?

Ding Bao Little Ding Bao. Pock-mark Liu Jr told me to come here. He says the old manager here asked him to find a waitress.

Wang Dashuan Take a good look around, miss. You think a **dump**① like this needs a waitress? But the old manager here's so desperate for money, he's always thinking up some crazy **scheme**②!

〔*Wang Lifa enters with a slow* ***gait***③. *He's still in good health, but* ***shabbily***④ *dressed.*〕

Wang Lifa Now, Dashuan, who taug you to **run down**⑤ your elders behind their backs? Who's full of crazy schemes? Take down the shutters! The teahouse should have opened long ago.

〔*Wang Dashuan goes to take down the shutters.*〕

Ding Bao Old manager, you look pretty fit!

Wang Lifa Yes. If there were some noodles with fried bean sauce around, I could **pack away**⑥ three huge bowls. Only there aren't any. Still in your teens, miss?

Ding Bao I'm seventeen.

Wang Lifa Only seventeen?

Ding Bao Yes. My mother was a widow, tried to bring me

利以后呀，政府硬说我爸爸给我们留下的一所小房子是逆产，给没收啦！妈妈气死了，我做了女招待！老掌柜，我到今天还不明白什么叫逆产，您知道吗?

王利发 姑娘，说话留点神！一句话说错了，什么都可以变成逆产！你看，这后边呀，是秦二爷的仓库，有人一瞪眼，说是逆产，就给没收啦！就是这么一回事！

〔王大拴回来。

丁　宝 老掌柜，您说对了！连我也是逆产，谁的胳臂粗，我就得侍候谁！他妈的，我才十七，就常想还不如死了呢！死了落个整尸首，干这一行，活着身上就烂了！

王大拴 爸，您真想要女招待吗?

王利发 我跟小刘麻子瞎聊来着！我一辈子老爱改良，看着生意这么不好，我着急！

王大拴 您着急，我也着急！可是，您就忘记老裕泰这个老字号了吗？六十多年的老字号，用女招待?

丁　宝 什么老字号啊！越老越不值钱！不信，我现在要是二十八岁，就是叫小小丁

Notes

① frown /fraun/ *v.* 皱眉头

② confiscate /'kɔnfiskeit/ *v.* 没收，充公

③ suck up to 巴结

up. After the war, the government insisted that the little house my father left us was traitor's property and took it away from us. The shock killed my mother. So I became a waitress. Old manager, I haven't a clue what traitor's property means. Do you know?

Wang Lifa Better watch your tongue, miss. One wrong word can make anything traitor's property. Take the place behind here. Used to be a warehouse of Master Qin. Then someone **frowned**① at it. Said it was traitor's property. It was **confiscated**②. Simple as that!

〔*Wang Dashuan comes back.*〕

Ding Bao You said it, old manager. Even I'm traitor's property! I have to **suck up to**③ whoever's the boss. Hell! I'm only seventeen but I often wish I was dead! At least my body would be my own! This job rots you away slowly.

Wang Dashuan Dad, do you really want to hire a waitress?

Wang Lifa I had a chat with Pock-mark Liu Jr about it. I've always been keen on reforming. And with business so bad, I'm worried.

Wang Dashuan Me too! But don't forget Yutai's good name. A respectable old name of sixty years' standing. Now hiring a waitress?

Ding Bao Good old name my foot! The older you become, the more worthless you are! You don't believe

宝，小丁宝贝，也没人看我一眼！

〔茶客甲、乙上。

王利发 二位早班儿！带着叶子哪？老大拿开水去！（王大拴下）二位，对不起，茶钱先付！

茶客甲 没听说过！

王利发 我开过几十年茶馆，也没听说过！可是，您圣明：茶叶、煤球儿都一会儿一个价钱，也许您正喝着茶，茶叶又长了价钱！您看，先收茶钱不是省得麻烦吗？

茶客乙 我看哪，不喝更省事！（同茶客甲下）

王大拴 （提来开水）怎么？走啦！

王利发 这你就明白了！

丁　宝 我要是过去说一声："来了？小子！"他们准给一块现大洋！

王利发 你呀，老大，比石头还顽固！

王大拴 （放下壶）好吧，我出去蹓蹓，这里出不来气！（下）

王利发 你出不来气，我还憋得慌呢！

〔小刘麻子上，穿着洋服，夹着皮包。

① sucker /ˈsʌkə/ *n.* ［美俚］傻瓜，容易上当的人

② shiny /ˈʃaini/ *a.* 有光泽的，发光的

③ mule /mjuːl/ *n.* 骡子

④ stuffy /ˈstʌfi/ *a.* 不通气的

me? If I were twenty-eig years old, I'd call myself Tiny Ding Bao or Ding Baby but I bet no one would look at me twice.

〔*Two customers enter.*〕

Wang Lifa You're early, gentlemen! Broug your own tea? Dashuan, get the water. 〔*Wang Dashuan goes.*〕 I'm sorry, but please pay in advance.

First customer I never heard such nonsense.

Wang Lifa I've been in this business fifty years now, and I've never heard such nonsense either. But, as you know, the prices of coal and such things are always going up. Perhaps while you're having your tea now, they'll go up again. So it saves a lot of trouble if you pay in advance.

Second customer Having no tea at all saves even more trouble!

〔*Exeunt the two customers.*〕

Wang Dashuan 〔*entering with hot water*〕 What? They've gone!

Wang Lifa Now do you see what I mean?

Ding Bao If I'd gone over and said, "Hi, you two **suckers**①! " they'd have handed over a **shiny**② silver dollar rig away.

Wang Lifa Dashuan, you're as stubborn as a **mule**③!

Wang Dashuan 〔*putting down the hot water*〕 Do what you like! I'll take a walk. It's too **stuffy**④ in here. 〔*Exit.*〕

Wang Lifa You find it stuffy? I can hardly breathe!

〔*Pock-mark Liu Jr enters. He is in western*

小刘麻子　小丁宝，你来啦？

丁　　宝　有你的话，谁敢不来呀！

小刘麻子　王掌柜，看我给你找来的小宝贝怎样？人材、岁数打扮、经验，样样出色！

王利发　就怕我用不起吧？

小刘麻子　没的事！她不要工钱！是吧，小丁宝？

王利发　不要工钱？

小刘麻子　老头儿，你都甭管，全听我的，我跟小丁宝有我们一套办法！是吧，小丁宝？

丁　　宝　要是没你那一套办法，怎会缺德呢！

小刘麻子　缺德？你算说对了！当初，我爸爸就是由这儿绑出去的；不信，你问王掌柜。是吧，王掌柜？

王利发　我亲眼得见！

小刘麻子　你看，小丁宝，我不乱吹吧？绑出去，就在马路中间，咔嚓一刀！是吧，老掌柜？

王利发　听得真真的！

小刘麻子　我不说假话吧？小丁宝！可是，我爸爸到底差点事。一辈子混的并不怎样。轮到我自己出头露面了，我

① briefcase /'briːfkeis/ *n.* 公文包

② smasher /'smæʃə/ *n.* 绝好的东西，漂亮的人

③ snag /snæg/ *n.* 暗礁，隐患

④ crooked /'krukid/ *a.* 弯曲的，邪恶的

⑤ shoot one's mouth off 信口开河，吹牛

⑥ whack /(h) wæk/ *n.* 重击，重打

⑦ nob /nɔb/ *n.* 头

clothes and carries a ***briefcase***[①]*.*〕

Pock-markliu jr Hi, Little Ding Bao, so you're here!

Ding Bao On your orders! How could I refuse?

Pock-markliu jr Manager Wang, what do you think of this little baby I've found for you? Looks, age, fashion, experience — she's a real **smasher**[②]!

Wang Lifa Only **snag**[③] is I can't afford her.

Pock-markliu jr No problem. She doesn't want any wages. Rig, baby?

Wang Lifa No wages?

Pock-markliu jr Leave it all to me, old man. Me and baby have got a way all worked out. Haven't we, baby?

Ding Bao Sure, without your **crooked**[④] ways, where would you be?

Pock-markliu jr Crooked? You've said it! So was my old man. He was nabbed rig here! If you don't believe me, ask Manager Wang. Wasn't that so?

Wang Lifa Saw it with my own eyes.

Pock-markliu jr See, baby, I'm not just **shooting my mouth off**[⑤] about something that never happened. He was dragged rig to the middle of the street, and with one big **whack**[⑥] of the sword, his **nob**[⑦] was chopped off. Rig, old manager?

Wang Lifa I heard that whack.

Pock-markliu jr So I wasn't just telling you stories, baby, was I? But my old man didn't have what it takes. All that work, but he still didn't get far. Now it's my

必得干的特别出色。(打开皮包，拿出计划书)看，小丁宝，看看我的计划!

丁　宝　我没那么大的工夫! 我看哪，我该回家，休息一天，明天来上工。

王利发　丁宝，我还没想好呢!

小刘麻子　王掌柜，我都替你想好啦! 不信，你等着看，明天早上，小丁宝在门口儿歪着头那么一站，马上就进来二百多茶座儿! 小丁宝，你听听我的计划，跟你有关系。

丁　宝　哼! 但愿跟我没关系!

小刘麻子　你呀，小丁宝，不够积极! 听着……

〔取电灯费的进来。

取电灯费的　掌柜的，电灯费!

王利发　电灯费? 欠几个月的啦?

取电灯费的　三个月的!

王利发　再等三个月，凑半年，我也还是没办法!

取电灯费的　那像什么话呢?

小刘麻子　地道真话嘛! 这儿属沈处长管。知道沈处长吧? 市党部的委员，宪兵司令部的处长! 你愿意收他的电费吗? 说!

① a wet blanket *n.* 扫兴的人或物

② municipal /mju(ː)'nisipəl/ *a.* 市的，市政的

turn, and I'm going to hit the big time! 〔*Opens briefcase and takes out the plan.*〕 Here, baby, take a look at my plan.

Ding Bao I've no time. I think I'l l take a day off and come back to work tomorrow.

Wang Lifa Ding Bao, I haven't made up my mind yet.

Pock-markliu jr Manager Wang, I've made it up for you! You'll see, tomorrow morning, baby will stand at the entrance giving everyone the eye. Before you know what's happened you'll have two hundred customers on your hands! Now, baby, better listen to my plan, because you're in it.

Ding Bao Huh! I was hoping I wasn't.

Pock-markliu jr What's the matter, baby, you're such **a wet blanket**①! Listen....

〔*The Electricity Bill Collector enters.*〕

The collector Hey, manager, your electricity bill.

Wang Lifa Electricity bill? I'm how many months behind?

The collector Three.

Wang Lifa Wait another three months and I'll be half a year. I still won't be able to pay you!

The collector That's nonsense!

Pock-markliu jr No, perfectly serious! This joint's under Director Shen's control. Ever heard of him? Member of the **municipal**② KMT Party committee, director of the Military Police. You want to collect his electricity bills? Come on, tell us?

取电灯费的 什么话呢，当然不收！对不起，我走错了门儿！（下）

小刘麻子 看，王掌柜，你不听我的行不行？你那套光绪年的办法太守旧了！

王利发 对！要不怎么说，人要活到老学到老呢！我还得多学！

小刘麻子 就是嘛！

〔小唐铁嘴进来，穿着绸子夹袍，新缎鞋。

小刘麻子 哎哟，他妈的是你，小唐铁嘴！

小唐铁嘴 哎哟，他妈的是你，小刘麻子！来，叫爷爷看看！（看前看后）你小子行，洋服穿的像那么一回事，由后边看哪，你比洋人还更像洋人！老王掌柜，我夜观天象，紫微星发亮，不久必有真龙天子出现，所以你看我跟小刘麻子，和这位……

小刘麻子 小丁宝，九城闻名！

小唐铁嘴 ……和这位小丁宝，才都这么才貌双全，文武带打，我们是应运而生，活在这个时代，真是如鱼得水！老掌柜，把脸转正了，我看看！好，好，印堂发亮，还有一步好运！来吧，给我碗

① once-over /ˈwʌnsəuvə/ *n.* 浏览一遍

② gear /giə/ *n.* ［英俚］（年轻人的）时髦服饰，派头

③ irrefutable /iˈrefjutəbl/ *a.* 不能反驳的，不能驳倒的

④ prodigy /ˈprɔdidʒi/ *n.* 不凡的人，神童

The collector What do you mean? No, no! Sorry, I guess I came to the wrong place. [*Exit.*]

Pock-markliu jr See, Manager Wang, you can't do without me! Your Qing-dynasty methods are way out of date!

Wang Lifa Rig. That's why as they say, one must live and learn. And I've a lot to learn!

Pock-markliu jr Now you're talking!

[*Tang the Oracle Jr enters. He wears a silk gown and new satin shoes.*]

Pock-markliu jr Oh, shit! It's you, Oracle Jr!

Tang the oracle jr Oh, shit! It's you, Pock-mark Jr! Come, let me give you the **once-over**[①]! [*Looking him over, front and back*] You little bastard! In that western **gear**[②], from behind you look more foreign than a foreigner. Old manager, I've been studying the stars and there's **irrefutable**[③] evidence that the true Son of Heaven will come amongst us very soon now. That's why **prodigies**[④] like me and Pock-mark Jr here and...

Pock-markliu jr Little Ding Bao — the talk of the town!

Tang the oracle jr Ah, yes, and Little Ding Bao have been sent into the world. Look at us, endowed with wit andbeauty, accomplished in letters and prowess — just rig for the times! And, boy, aren't we going to enjoy it! Old manager, turn your face

喝吧!

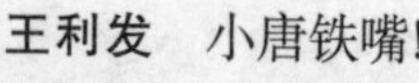

王利发　小唐铁嘴!

小唐铁嘴　别再叫唐铁嘴，我现在叫唐天师!

小刘麻子　谁封你做了天师?

小唐铁嘴　待两天你就知道了。

王利发　天师，可别忘了，你爸爸白喝了我一辈子的茶，这可不能世袭!

小唐铁嘴　王掌柜，等我穿上八卦仙衣的时候，你会后悔刚才说了什么!你等着吧!

小刘麻子　小唐，待会儿请你去喝咖啡，小丁宝作陪，你先听我说点正经事，好不好?

小唐铁嘴　王掌柜，你就不想想，天师今天白喝你点茶，将来会给你个县知事做做吗?好吧，小刘你说!

小刘麻子　我这儿刚跟小丁宝说，我有个伟大的计划!

小唐铁嘴　好!洗耳恭听!

小刘麻子　我要组织一个“拖拉撕”。这是个美国字，也许你不懂，翻成北京话就是“包圆儿”。

Notes

① spell /spel/ *n.* 一段时间

② hereditary /hiˈreditəri/ *a.* 世袭的，遗传的

③ treat sb. to sth. 宴飨，款待

④ magistrate /ˈmædʒistrit/ *n.* 地方行政长官

⑤ tremendous /triˈmendəs/ *a.* 巨大的，惊人的

⑥ trust /trʌst/ *n.* 托拉斯，企业联合

⑦ dialect /ˈdaiəlekt/ *n.* 方言

here. I'll read your features. Good, good, a fine forehead! You're in for a **spell**① of good luck! Now what about a cup of tea?

Wang Lifa Oracle Jr!

Tang the oracle jr Don't call me Oracle any more. My new title is Tang the Heavenly Teacher.

Pock-markliu jr Who gave you that?

Tang the oracle jr You'll hear about it in a few days.

Wang Lifa All rig, Heavenly Teacher, but don't forget, your father had free tea off me all his life! That's not going to be **hereditary**②, I hope!

Tang the oracle jr Manager Wang, when I have put on my special robes, you'll regret what you've just said. You just wait!

Pock-markliu jr Tang, my old pal, I'll **treat you to a coffee**③ later with baby here to keep us company. But first I want to tell you something important.

Tang the oracle jr Manager Wang, has it never entered your head that by offering me some free tea now I may make you a county **magistrate**④ later? Now, Liu, my old buddy, say your piece.

Pock-markliu jr I was just saying to baby here, I've got a **tremendous**⑤ plan.

Tang the oracle jr I'm all ears.

Pock-markliu jr I'm going to organize a **trust**⑥. That's an American word, so perhaps you don't understand it. In Beijing **dialect**⑦ it means "it's all yours".

小唐铁嘴 我懂！就是说，所有的姑娘全由你包办。

小刘麻子 对，你的脑力不坏！小丁宝，听着，这跟你有密切关系！甚至于跟王掌柜也有关系！

王利发 我这儿听着呢！

小刘麻子 我要把舞女、明娼、暗娼、吉普女郎和女招待全组织起来，成立那么一个大"拖拉撕"。

小唐铁嘴 （闭着眼问）官方上疏通好了没有？

小刘麻子 当然！沈处长做董事长，我当总经理！

小唐铁嘴 我呢？

小刘麻子 你要是能琢磨出个好名字来，请你做顾问！

小唐铁嘴 车马费不要法币！

小刘麻子 每月送几块美钞！

小唐铁嘴 往下说！

小刘麻子 业务方面包括：买卖部、转运部、训练部、供应部，四大部。谁买姑娘，还是谁卖姑娘；由上海调运到天津，还是由汉口调运到重庆；训练吉普女郎，还是训练女招待；是供应美国军队，还是各级官员，都由公司统一承办，保证人人满意。你看怎样？

① prostitute /'prɔstitjuːt/ *n.* 妓女
② tart/tɑːt/ *n.* 妓女

③ greenback /'griːnbæk/ *n.* 美钞
④ fire away 开始

⑤ personnel /ˌpəːsə'nel/ *n.* 人员，职员

Tang the oracle jr Of course, I see it. It means you want to take care of all the girls.

Pock-markliu jr Rig! That brain of yours really works! Baby, listen carefully. You're a part of this too. Even the old manager here's included.

Wang Lifa That's why I'm listening.

Pock-markliu jr I'm going to organize all the dance-hall girls, **prostitutes**① in the brothels and **tarts**② on the street, jeep girls and waitresses into a huge trust.

Tang the oracle jr 〔*with his eyes closed*〕 Got all the official backing you need?

Pock-markliu jr Sure! Director Shen will be chairman of the board. I'll be general manager.

Tang the oracle jr What about me?

Pock-markliu jr If you can think up a good name for it, you'll be our adviser!

Tang the oracle jr I won't take national currency bills for my fees.

Pock-markliu jr Only **greenbacks**③ every month!

Tang the oracle jr **Fire away**④!

Pock-markliu jr The business will have four departments: Purchase and Sales, Transport, Training, and Service. Whoever wants to buy or sell girls, whether they're to be transported from Shanghai to Tianjin or from Hankou to Chongqing, whether it's training jeep girls or waitresses, or girls serving US army **personnel**⑤ or our own officials, all this will be taken care of by our firm.

小唐铁嘴　太好！太好！在道理上，这合乎统制一切的原则。在实际上，这首先能满足美国兵的需要，对国家有利！

小刘麻子　好吧，你就给想个好名字吧！想个文雅的，像"柳叶眉，杏核眼，樱桃小口一点点"那种诗那么文雅的！

小唐铁嘴　嗯——"拖拉撕"，"拖拉撕"……不雅！拖进来，拉进来，不听话就撕成两半儿，倒好像是绑票儿撕票儿，不雅！

小刘麻子　对，是不大雅！可那是美国字，吃香啊！

小唐铁嘴　还是联合公司响亮、大方！

小刘麻子　有你这么一说！什么联合公司呢？

丁　宝　缺德公司就挺好！

小刘麻子　小丁宝，谈正经事，不许乱说！你好好干，将来你有做女招待总教官的希望！

小唐铁嘴　看这个怎样——花花联合公司？姑娘是什么？鲜花嘛！要姑娘就得多

Notes

① guarantee /ˌɡærən'tiː/ *v.* 保证，担保

② theoretically /θiə'retikəli/ *ad.* 理论上的

③ GI /dʒiː'ai/ 〔美〕*a.* 美国军事人员的

④ willow /'wiləu/ *n.* 柳树

⑤ almond /'ɑːmənd/ *n.* 杏仁

⑥ dainty /'deinti/ *a.* 优美的，讲究的

⑦ kidnap /'kidnæp/ *v.* 绑架，诱拐

⑧ incorporated /in'kɔːpəreitid/ *a.* 组成公司的

⑨ blossom /'blɔsəm/ *n.* 花，花朵

Total satisfaction **guaranteed**[1]. What do you think of that?

Tang the oracle jr Marvellous! Marvellous! **Theoretically**[2], it follows the principle of getting everything under control. In practice it satisfies the needs of`the **GI**'s[3], and that's in the interest of the state.

Pock-markliu jr Then, think of a nice name. Something real classy, like "**Willow**[4]-leaf eyebrows, **almond**[5]-shaped eyes; Cherry red lips of a **dainty**[6] size". Poetic, you know.

Tang the oracle jr H'm... Trust, trust... No, that's not classy at all. In Beijing dialect, the word sounds like "Pull them in and tear them to pieces"! Sound too much like **kidnapping**[7] to be classy.

Pock-markliu jr It may not sound classy, but it's an American word and that's fashionable.

Tang the oracle jr I still feel that "something **incorporated**[8]" sounds better. It's got more taste.

Pock-markliu jr You've got a point there.But what "incorporated"?

Ding Bao How about "Crooked Incorporated"?

Pock-markliu jr Look, baby, this is serious! Don't be so smart! Do your job well and there's a good chance you'll become the chief instructor of the waitresses.

Tang the oracle jr What about this: "Two **Blossoms**[9] Incorporated"? What do pretty girls make you think of?

花钱，花呀花呀，所以花花！“青是山，绿是水，花花世界”，又有典故，出自《武家坡》！好不好？

小刘麻子 小唐，我谢谢你，谢谢你！（热烈握手）我马上找沈处长去研究一下，他一赞成，你的顾问就算当上了！（收拾皮包，要走）

王利发 我说，丁宝的事到底怎么办？

小刘麻子 没告诉你不用管吗？“拖拉撕”统办一切，我先在这里试验试验。

丁　宝 你不是说喝咖啡去吗？

小刘麻子 问小唐去不去？

小唐铁嘴 你们先去吧，我还在这儿等个人。

小刘麻子 咱们走吧，小丁宝！

丁　宝 明天见，老掌柜！再见，天师！（同小刘麻子下）

小唐铁嘴 王掌柜，拿报来看看！

王利发 那，我得慢慢地找去。二年前的还许有几张！

小唐铁嘴 废话！

〔进来三位茶客：明师傅、邹福远和卫福喜。明师傅独坐，邹福远与卫福喜同坐。王利发都认识，向大家

Blossoms! If people want these girls, they'll spend lots of money and your business will — what? Blossom! The two blossoms! And in traditional opera there are many references to two blossoms. So what do you think?

Pock-markliu jr Tang, old mate, I thank you. Thanks a lot! [*Warm handshake.*] I'll go rig now and see Director Shen and discuss it with him. If he agrees, you'll definitely be our adviser. [*Puts the briefcase in order, ready to go.*]

Wang Lifa Hey, what about Little Ding Bao?

Pock-markliu jr Trust me! The trust will have everything under control. I'll try it out here first.

Ding Bao Didn't you say something about coffee?

Pock-markliu jr See if Tang's coming.

Tang the oracle jr You go ahead. I'm expecting someone here.

Pock-markliu jr Then let's get going, baby.

Ding Bao Bye-bye, old manager. Bye, Heavenly Teacher. [*Goes off with Pock-mark Liu Jr.*]

Tang the oracle jr Old manager, where's the paper?

Wang Lifa I'll have to look for it. Perhaps some copies from two years ago are still lying around somewhere.

Tang the oracle jr Oh, stop talking nonsense!

[*Three customers enter: Chef Ming, Zou Fuyuan and Wei Fuxi. The chef finds a place for himself, while Zou and Wei sit together.*

点头。

王利发 哥儿们，对不起啊，茶钱先付！

明师傅 没错儿，老哥哥！

王利发 唉！“茶钱先付”，说着都烫嘴！（忙着沏茶）

邹福远 怎样啊？王掌柜！晚上还添评书不添啊？

王利发 试验过了，不行！光费电，不上座儿！

邹福远 对！您看，前天我在会仙馆，开三侠四义五霸十雄十三杰九老十五小，大破凤凰山，百鸟朝凤，棍打凤腿，您猜上了多少座儿？

王利发 多少？那点书现在除了您，没有人会说！

邹福远 您说的在行！可是，才上了五个人，还有俩听蹭儿的！

卫福喜 师哥，无论怎么说，你比我强！我又闲了一个多月啦！

邹福远 可谁叫你跳了行，改唱戏了呢？

卫福喜 我有嗓子，有扮相嘛！

邹福远 可是上了台，你又不好好地唱！

Notes

① gallant /ˈgælənt/ *a.* 英勇的，壮丽的

② worthies /ˈwəːðiz/ *n.* 要人；大人物

③ storm /stɔːm/ *v.* 猛攻，捣毁

④ pay homage to 向……表示敬意

⑤ phoenix /ˈfiːniks/ *n.* 凤凰

⑥ connoisseur /ˌkɔniˈsəː/ *n.* 鉴定家，内行

Knowing them all, Wang Lifa greets them.]

Wang Lifa My friends, I'm sorry to ask you, but please pay in advance.

Chef Ming We all know that, old man.

Wang Lifa Pay in advance! I'm really ashamed to say it. [*Busies himself preparing the tea.*]

Zou Fuyuan What about it, manager? How about story-telling as an added attraction in the evenings?

Wang Lifa I tried, but it was no good. Only increased the electricity bill, but not the number of customers!

Zou Fuyuan Exactly! Take me. Day before yesterday, at Huixian Teahouse, I told the story of how the three **gallants**①, four **worthies**②, five braves, ten heroes, thirteen celebrities, nine elders and fifteen youngsters **stormed**③ Phoenix Mountain, how the hundred birds **paid homage to**④ the **phoenix**⑤, and how the phoenix's leg was hurt. Guess how many came to listen to me?

Wang Lifa How many? You're the only one left who can tell that story.

Zou Fuyuan A true **connoisseur**⑥! But, only five turned up and two of them didn't even pay.

Wei Fuxi Well, anyway, you're better off than me. Another month now and I've had no work.

Zou Fuyuan But why did you give up story-telling for Beijing opera?

Wei Fuxi I've got the voice and the looks.

Zou Fuyuan But on stage, you don't throw yourself into the part!

卫福喜 妈的唱一出戏，挣不上三个杂和面儿饼子的钱，我干吗卖力气呢？我疯啦？

邹福远 唉！福喜，咱们哪，全叫流行歌曲跟《纺棉花》给顶垮喽！我是这么看，咱们死，咱们活着，还在其次，顶伤心的是咱们这点玩艺儿，再过几年都得失传！咱们对不起祖师爷！常言道：邪不侵正。这年头就是邪年头，正经东西全得连根儿烂！

王利发 唉！（转至明师傅处）明师傅，可老没来啦！

明师傅 出不来喽！包监狱里的伙食呢！

王利发 您！就凭您，办一二百桌满汉全席的手儿，去给他们蒸窝窝头？

明师傅 那有什么办法呢，现而今就是狱里人多呀，满汉全席？我连家伙都卖喽！

〔方六拿着几张画儿进来。

明师傅 六爷，这儿！六爷，那两桌家伙怎样啦？我等钱用！

Notes

① maize /meiz/ *n.* 玉米
② bun /bʌn/ *n.* 小面包，馒头
③ fag out 累坏
④ operetta /ˌɔpəˈretə/ *n.* 小歌剧
⑤ vanquish /ˈvæŋkwiʃ/ *v.* 打败，征服
⑥ in charge of 负责
⑦ jailbird /ˈdʒeilbəːd/ *n.* 囚犯，累犯
⑧ in clink 坐牢
⑨ utensil /ju(ː)ˈtensl/ *n.* 器具
⑩ scroll /skrəul/ *n.* 卷轴，画卷

Wei Fuxi Damn it, for singing the whole opera, I don't get enough to buy three **maize**① **buns**②! Why be **fagged out**③? You think I'm off my head?

Zou Fuyuan 〔*sighs*〕 Well, Fuxi, it looks as though we've been beaten by pop songs and trashy **operettas** ④ like Spinning Cotton. The way I feel about it, it doesn't matter if you or I live or die, but it breaks my heart to think that what's left of our art will die out in a few years! We've failed our legendary founders. It's an old saying that evil will never **vanquish** ⑤ good. But these are evil times, and everything good is rotting away at the roots!

Wang Lifa Ah! 〔*Turning to Chef Ming*〕 Chef Ming, I haven't seen you for ages.

Chef Ming Can't get about so much now. I'm now **in charge of**⑥ the food at the prison.

Wang Lifa What? You? But you used to cater for those posh imperial-style banquets with more than a hundred tables. Now you're cooking for **jailbirds**⑦!

Chef Ming But what can I do? Nowadays you can only find so many mouths to feed **in clink** ⑧. Imperial-style banquets indeed! I've even sold off my cooking **utensils**⑨.

〔*Fang Liu enters, with some traditional painting* ***scrolls***⑩.〕

Chef Ming Mr Fang, come over here, please. What happened to my two dinner services? I need the money!

方　六　明师傅，您挑一张画儿吧!

明师傅　啊? 我要画儿干吗呢?

方　六　这可画得不错! 六大山人、董弱梅画的!

明师傅　画得天好，当不了饭吃啊!

方　六　他把画儿交给我的时候，直掉眼泪!

① hand over 移交，接管

明师傅　我把家伙交给你的时候，也直掉眼泪!

方　六　谁掉眼泪，谁吃炖肉，我都知道! 要不怎么我累心呢! 你当是干我们这一行，专凭打打小鼓就行哪?

明师傅　六爷，人总有颗人心哪，你还能坑老朋友吗?

② rook /ruk/ *v.* 骗

③ peanut /ˈpiːnʌt/ *n.* 花生

方　六　一共不是才两桌家伙吗? 小事儿，别再提啦，再提就好像不大懂交情了!

〔车当当敲着两块洋钱，进来。

④ rattle /ˈrætl/ *v.* 使……嘎嘎响

车当当　谁买两块? 买两块吧? 天师，照顾照顾? （小唐铁嘴不语）

王利发　当当! 别处转转吧，我连现大洋什么模样都忘了!

车当当　那，你老人家就细细看看吧! 白看，不

Fang Liu	Chef, pick one of these scrolls instead?
Chef Ming	But what would I do with a scroll.
Fang Liu	It's so well painted. Even better than the original!
Chef Ming	It may be the best in the world, but it won't fill my belly.
Fang Liu	When the owner **handed them over**① to me, he was in tears.
Chef Ming	So was I when I handed over my dinner services!
Fang Liu	I know damn well who's in tears and who's stuffing his guts! That's why I'm always so upset. Don't imagine people in my trade have no heart and just go around buying and selling things.
Chef Ming	Mr Fang, everyone has at least a little humanity. You're surely not going to **rook**② an old friend, I hope?
Fang Liu	Only two dinner services, wasn't it? **Peanuts**③! Please don't mention them again. Doesn't sound friendly somehow!
	〔*Che Dangdang enters,* **rattling**④ *two silver dollars together.*〕
Che Dangdang	Who'll buy silver dollars? Anyone want to buy silver dollars? Heavenly Teacher, won't you favour me?
	〔*Tang the Oracle Jr ignores him.*〕
Wang Lifa	Dangdang, try your luck somewhere else. I can't even remember what silver dollars look like.
Che Dangdang	Have a good look then, old man. Free of charge!

用买票!（往桌上扔钱)

〔庞四奶奶进来，带着春梅。庞四奶奶的手上戴满各种戒指，打扮得像个女妖精。卖杂货的老杨跟进来。

小唐铁嘴 娘娘!

方　六
车当当 娘娘!

庞四奶奶 天师!

小唐铁嘴 侍候娘娘!（让庞四奶奶坐，给她倒茶)

庞四奶奶 （看车当当要出去）当当，你等等!

车当当 嗻!

老　杨 （打开货箱）娘娘，看看吧!

庞四奶奶 唱唱那套词儿，还倒怪有个意思!

老　杨 是!美国针、美国线、美国牙膏、美国消炎片。还有口红、雪花膏、玻璃袜子细毛线。箱子小，货物全，就是不卖原子弹!

庞四奶奶 哈哈哈!（挑了两双袜子）春梅，拿着!当当，你跟老杨算账吧!

Notes

① encrust /in'krʌst/ *v.* 包以外壳

② nauseating /'nɔːsieitiŋ/ *a.* 使人恶心的

③ in one's wake 紧随

④ jingle /'dʒiŋgl/ *n.* 叮当声

⑤ yankee /'jæŋki/ *n.* 美国公民，美国佬

⑥ patent /'peitənt/ *a.* 专利的，新奇的

⑦ potion /'pəuʃən/ *n.* 一服，一剂

⑧ lotion /'ləuʃən/ *n.* 洗涤剂，洗液

⑨ nylon /'nailən/ *n.* 尼龙

⑩ sheer /ʃiə/ *a.* 绝对的，全然的

⑪ atom /'ætəm/ *n.* 原子

[*Drops the silver dollars on to the table.*]

[*Madame Pang enters with her bondmaid Chunmei. Her fingers* **encrusted**[①] *with all kinds of rings, the woman is overdressed to a* **nauseating**[②] *degree. Yang, the pedlar, enters* **in her wake**[③].]

Tang the oracle jr　Your Imperial Majesty!

Fang Liu
Che Dangdang　Your Imperial Majesty!

Mme Pang　Heavenly Teacher!

Tang the oracle jr　At your service. [*Helps Madame Pang to a seat, pours tea for her.*]

Mme Pang　[*as Che Dangdang prepares to go*] Dangdang, just a minute!

Che Dangdang　Yes, ma'am!

Yang　[*opening up his chest of goods*] Have a look, Your Imperial Majesty.

Mme Pang　Let's hear that **jingle**[④] of yours. It just kills me!

Yang　Yes, ma'am.[*Recites.*]

Yankee[⑤] needles, Yankee thread;
Toothpaste white and lipstick red.
Patent[⑥] **potions**[⑦], facial **lotions**[⑧];
Nylons[⑨] **sheer**[⑩], you'll find here.
In my small box, all goods are fine
But **atom**[⑪] bombs just ain't my line!

Mme Pang　[*laughing, picks two pairs of nylon stockings*] Chunmei, put them away. Dangdang, settle

车当当　娘娘，别那么办哪!

庞四奶奶　我给你拿的本钱，利滚利，你欠我多少啦?天师，查账!

小唐铁嘴　是!（掏小本）

车当当　天师，你甭操心，我跟老杨算去!

老　杨　娘娘，您行行好吧!他能给我钱吗?

庞四奶奶　老杨，他坑不了你，都有我呢!

老　杨　是!（向众）还有哪位照顾照顾?（又要唱）美国针……

庞四奶奶　听够了!走!

老　杨　是!

美国针、美国线，

我要不走是浑蛋!

走，当当!（同车当当下）

方　六　（过来）娘娘，我得到一堂景泰蓝的五供儿，东西老，地道，也便宜，坛上用顶体面，您看看吧?

Notes

① compound /'kɔmpaund/ *a.* 复合的
compound interest 复利

② cloisonne /klɔizə'nei/ *n.* 景泰蓝磁器

③ incense /in'sens/ *n.* 香

④ antique /æn'tiːk/ *n.* 古物，古董

⑤ dirt cheap 便宜透顶

⑥ altar /'ɔːltə/ *n.* （教堂内的）圣坛，祭坛

the accounts with Yang.

Che Dangdang Oh, Your Imperial Majesty, don't do that to me.

Mme Pang But I lent you money, so what do you owe me now, at **compound**[1] interest? Heavenly Teacher, check the accounts!

Tang the oracle jr Immediately. 〔*Takes out a small notebook.*〕

Che Dangdang Heavenly Teacher, don't bother! I'll settle everything with Yang.

Yang Your Imperial Majesty, have pity on me. I'll never get that money.

Mme Pang Don't worry, Yang. I'll see to it that he won't cheat you.

Yang Yes, ma'am.〔*To others present*〕Anyone else want to buy something? 〔*Begins his recitation again.*〕Yankee needles...

Mme Pang Enough! Beat it!

Yang Sure. 〔*Recites.*〕

Yankee needles, Yankee thread;
If I don't go, I'm a silly fathead!
Let's go, Dangdang. 〔Exeunt Yang and Che Dangdang.〕

Fang Liu 〔*coming over*〕

Your Imperial Majesty, I managed to get hold of a set of **cloisonne**[2] **incense**[3] burners, five pieces in all. **Antiques**[4]! The real thing! **Dirt cheap**[5] too. Just rig for the **altar**[6] of our secret society. Why not have a peep at them?

庞四奶奶 请皇上看看吧!

方　六 是! 皇上不是快登基了吗? 我先给您道喜! 我马上取去, 送到坛上! 娘娘多给美言几句, 我必有份人心! (往外走)

明师傅 六爷, 我的事呢?!

方　六 你先给我看着那几张画! (下)

明师傅 你等等! 坑我两桌家伙, 我还有把切菜刀呢! (追下)

庞四奶奶 王掌柜, 康妈妈在这儿哪? 请她出来!

小唐铁嘴 我去! (跑到后门) 康老太太, 您来一下!

王利发 什么事?

小唐铁嘴 朝廷大事!

〔康顺子上。

康顺子 干什么呀?

庞四奶奶 (迎上去) 婆母! 我是您的四侄媳妇, 来接您, 快坐下吧! (拉康顺子坐下)

康顺子 四侄媳妇?

Notes

① coronation /kɔrə'neiʃ(ə)n/ *n.* 加冕礼

② chopper /'tʃɔpə/ *n.* 斧头, 切肉大刀

③ pursue /pə'sjuː/ *v.* 追捕, 追求

④ momentous /məu'mentəs/ *a.* 重要的, 重大的

⑤ effusively /i'fjuːsivli/ *ad.* 喷发地, 感情奔放地

Mme Pang Show them to the emperor.

Fang Liu Of course! I hear that our emperor is going to have his **coronation**① soon. My congratulations! I'll go and get the incense burners now and take them to the altar. If Your Imperial Majesty puts in a good word for me, I won't forget it. 〔*On his way out.*〕

Chef Ming Mr Fang, what about our bit of business?

Fang Liu Keep an eye on those scrolls for the time being. 〔*Exit.*〕

Chef Ming Hey! Wait! Do me out of my dinner services, would you? Remember I've still got my meat **chopper**② left!

〔***Pursuing***③ *Fang, he goes off.*〕

Mme Pang Manager Wang, is Aunt Kang around? Please ask her to come here.

Tang the oracle jr I'll do it. 〔*Running to the door at the back*〕 Old Mrs Kang, please come here.

Wang Lifa What's all this about?

Tang the oracle jr **Momentous**④ affairs of state!

〔*Kang Shunz enters.*〕

Kang Shunz What do you want?

Mme Pang 〔*welcoming her* ***effusively***⑤〕 Mother-in-law! I'm the wife of your fourth nephew. I've come to take you home. Please sit down. 〔*Forces Kang Shunz into a chair.*〕

Kang Shunz Wife of my fourth nephew?

庞四奶奶　是呀，您离开庞家的时候，我还没过门哪。

康顺子　我跟庞家一刀两断啦，找我干吗？

庞四奶奶　您的四侄子海顺呀，是三皇道的大坛主，国民党的大党员，又是沈处长的把兄弟，快做皇上啦，您不喜欢吗？

康顺子　快做皇上？

庞四奶奶　啊！龙袍都做好啦，就快在西山登基！

康顺子　在西山？

小唐铁嘴　老太太，西山一带有八路军。庞四爷在那一带登基，消灭八路，南京能够不愿意吗？

① wipe out 彻底摧毁，消灭

庞四奶奶　四爷呀都好，近来可是有点贪酒好色。他已经弄了好几个小老婆！

② booze /buːz/ *v.* 豪饮

小唐铁嘴　娘娘，三宫六院七十二嫔妃，可有书可查呀！

庞四奶奶　你不是娘娘，怎么知道娘娘的委屈！老太太，我是这么想：您要是跟我一条心，我叫您做老太后，咱们俩

Mme Pang That's rig. But when you left the Pangs, I hadn't married into the family then.

Kang Shunz I've finished with the Pangs. Why look me up?

Mme Pang Your fourth nephew, Haishun, is the high priest of the "Tri-emperor" Society, a big nob in the Kuomintang and a sworn brother of Director Shen. Soon he's going to be made emperor! Isn't that fantastic?

Kang Shunz Going to be made emperor?

Mme Pang Yes. His imperial dragon robes are all ready. The coronation will soon take place in the Western Hills.

Kang Shunz The Western Hills?

Tang the oracle jr Old lady, don't you know the Communist Eigh Route Army units are in the Western Hills? When Master Pang becomes emperor, he'll **wipe out**① those Commies. Of course the Nanjing government is all for it!

Mme Pang I've nothing against the master, except that he's taken to **boozing**② and women lately. Got himself several concubines already!

Tang the oracle jr But, Your Majesty, an emperor should have seventy-two concubines apart from his official wives. That's all laid out in the old books.

Mme Pang You're not an empress. How can you know what an empress has to suffer? Now, old lady, I've got an idea. If you side with me, I'll

一齐管着皇上，我这个娘娘不就好做一点了吗？老太太，您跟我去，吃好的喝好的，兜儿里老带着那么几块当当响的洋钱，够多么好啊!

康顺子 我要是不跟你去呢?

庞四奶奶 啊？不去？（要翻脸）

小唐铁嘴 让老太太想想，想想!

康顺子 用不着想，我不会再跟庞家的人打交道！四媳妇，你做你的娘娘，我做我的苦老婆子，谁也别管谁！刚才你要瞪眼睛，你当我怕你吗？我在外边也混了这么多年，磨练出来点了，谁跟我瞪眼，我会伸手打!（立起，往后走）

小唐铁嘴 老太太！老太太!

康顺子 （立住，转身对小唐铁嘴）你呀，小伙子，挺起腰板来，去挣碗干净饭吃，不好吗？（下）

庞四奶奶 （移怒于王利发）王掌柜，过来！你去跟那个老婆子说说，说好了，我送给你一袋子白面！说不好，我砸了你的茶馆！天师，走!

Notes

① thumb /θʌm/ *n.* 拇指

② outburst /'autbəːst/ *n.* 爆发，突发

③ throw a scene 大吵大闹

④ loafer /'ləufə/ *n.* 游手好闲的人，懒人

⑤ vent /vent/ *v.* 发泄

⑥ wrath /rɔːθ/ *n.* 愤怒，激怒

⑦ hag /hæg/ *n.* 巫婆，老丑婆

make you the empress dowager. Then between us we'll have the emperor under our **thumbs**①. That'll make my life a lot easier. Come with me, old lady, and I promise you the best food and drink, plus some silver dollars to jingle in your pocket! What a posh life!

Kang Shunz And if I refuse?

Mme Pang What? Refuse? 〔*On the point of an* **outburst**②.〕

Tang the oracle jr Give her time to think it over. Give her time!

Kang Shunz I don't need it. I'm finished with the Pangs for ever! Wife of my nephew, you carry on being an empress and I'll carry on being a poor old woman. Let's keep out of each other's hair! Just now you were about to **throw a scene**③. You think that'd scare me? After all these years on my own, I know how to take care of myself. Try something, and I'll teach you a lesson! 〔*Stands up and walks to the rear.*〕

Tang the oracle jr Old lady! Old lady!

Kang Shunz 〔*stops, turns to Tang the Oracle Jr*〕 As for you, you young **loafer**④, why don't you stand on your two feet and make a decent living? 〔*Exit.*〕

Mme Pang 〔***venting***⑤ *her* ***wrath***⑥ *on Wang Lifa*〕 Manager Wang, come here! Go and talk some sense into that old **hag**⑦! Persuade her, and I'll give you a bag of flour. If not, I'll have your teahouse smashed up! Heavenly Teacher, let's go!

小唐铁嘴　王掌柜，我晚上还来，听你的回话!

王利发　万一我下半天就死了呢?

庞四奶奶　呸! 你还不该死吗? （与小唐铁嘴、春梅同下）

王利发　哼!

邹福远　师弟，你看这算哪一出? 哈哈哈!

卫福喜　我会二百多出戏，就是不懂这一出! 你知道那个娘儿们的出身吗?

邹福远　我还能不知道! 东霸天的女儿，在娘家就生过……得，别细说，我看这群浑蛋都有点回光反照，长不了!

〔王大拴回来。

王利发　看着点，老大。我到后面商量点事! (下)

小二德子　(在外边大吼一声) 闪开了! （进来）大拴哥，沏壶顶好的，我有钱! (掏出四块现洋，一块一块地放下) 给算算，刚才花了一块，这儿还有四块，五毛打一个，我一共打了几个?

① kick the bucket 一命呜呼，死了

② good riddance 可庆幸地摆脱，拔了眼中钉

③ cow /kau/ *n.* ［俚］肥胖而不整洁的女人

④ give birth to 生（孩子）

⑤ fling /fliŋ/ *n.* 放肆，放纵

⑥ thunderous /ˈθʌndərəs/ *a.* 雷鸣般的

Tang the oracle jr Manager Wang, I'll be back for your answer this evening.

Wang Lifa Suppose I **kick the bucket**① this afternoon?

Mme Pang Pah! Then **good riddance**②! 〔*Goes off with Tang the Oracle Jr and Chunmei.*〕

Wang Lifa Huh!

Zou Fuyuan Now, have you ever seen a better act? Ha! Ha!

Wei Fuxi I know more than two hundred operas, but I've never come across this one before. Where does the old **cow**③ come from?

Zou Fuyuan Everyone knows! Her father's a local gangster, who runs the eastern district in Beijing. She, herself, before she got married **gave birth to**④... er, well, let's not go into details! Looks as though those thugs are having their last **fling**⑤ before they go under. It won't be long now! 〔*Wang Dashuan comes back.*〕

Wang Lifa Keep an eye on things, Dashuan, I have to go and talk over something. 〔*Exit.*〕

Erdez Jr 〔*with a* ***thunderous***⑥ *shout before entering*〕 Get out the way! 〔*Enters.*〕Brother Dashuan, a pot of the very best. I'm in the money today! 〔*Takes out four silver dollars and puts them down one by one.*〕 Work it out for me. Just spent one dollar. Got four left. Half a dollar each, how many I done in?

王大拴 十个。

小二德子 (用手指算)对!前天四个,昨天六个,可不是十个!大拴哥,你拿两块吧!没钱,我白喝你的茶;有钱,就给你!你拿吧!(吹一块,放在耳旁听听)这块好,就一块当两块吧,给你!

王大拴 (没接钱)小二德子,什么生意这么好啊?现大洋不容易看到啊!

小二德子 念书去了!

王大拴 把"一"字都念成扁担,你念什么书啊?

小二德子 (拿起桌上的壶来,对着壶嘴喝了一气,低声说)市党部派我去的,法政学院。没当过这么美的差事,太美,太过瘾!比在天桥好的多!打一个学生,五毛现洋!昨天揍了几个来着?

王大拴 六个。

小二德子 对!里边还有两个女学生!一拳一拳地下去,太美,太过瘾!大拴哥,你摸摸,摸摸!(伸臂)铁筋洋灰的!用这个揍男女学生,你想想,美不美?

王大拴 他们就那么老实,乖乖地叫你打?

Notes

① racket /'rækit/ *n.* 行业,工作

② gulp /gʌlp/ *v.* 吞,呛

③ spout /spaut/ *n.* 喷口

④ institute /'institjuːt/ *n.* 学会,学院

⑤ pushover /'pʊʃəuvə(r)/ *n.* (俚)易于征服或控制的人

⑥ bum /bʌm/ *n.* 游荡者,懒鬼

⑦ punch /pʌntʃ/ *n.* 殴打

⑧ flex /fleks/ *v.* 弯曲,伸缩

⑨ biceps /'baiseps/ *n.* 二头肌

⑩ reinforced /ˌriːin'fɔːsd/ *a.* 被加强了的,加筋的

⑪ concrete /'kɔnkriːt/ *n.* 水泥,混凝土

Wang Dashuan Ten.

Erdez Jr 〔*counting on his fingers*〕 Rig! Four the day before yesterday, six yesterday. That's ten all rig. Brother Dashuan, here's a couple of dollars. When I'm broke, I drink your tea free. When I'm in the money, I pay you. Take 'em! 〔*Picks one up, blows on it, then holds it to his ear.*〕That's a good 'un. Good enough for two! Take it!

Wang Dashuan 〔*without accepting the money*〕 Erdez Jr, what's your **racket**①? Silver dollars don't grow on trees!

Erdez Jr I'm studying at the uni!

Wang Dashuan But you can't even read the character for "one"! How come you're at the university?

Erdez Jr 〔*picks up the teapot and* ***gulps***② *it down from the* ***spout***③. *In a whisper*〕 The Beijing KMT Party headquarters sent me to the **Institute**④ of Law and Politics. What a **pushover**⑤! A dream! Better than mixing with those **bums**⑥ in Tianqiao. Half a dollar for every student I did in. How many did I get yesterday?

Wang Dashuan Six.

Erdez Jr Rig. Including two chicks. One **punch**⑦ after another. A dream! Brother Dashuan, feel this. Feel it! 〔***Flexing***⑧ *his* ***biceps***⑨〕 **Reinforced**⑩ **concrete**⑪! Imagine that on the students. Smashing, eh?

Wang Dashuan Of course they take it all lying down?

小二德子　我专找老实的打呀！你当我是傻子哪？

王大拴　小二德子，听我说，打人不对！

小二德子　可也难说！你看教党义的那个教务长，上课先把手枪拍在桌上，我不过抡抡拳头，没动手枪啊！

王大拴　什么教务长啊，流氓！

小二德子　对！流氓！不对，那我也是流氓喽！大拴哥，你怎么绕着脖子骂我呢？大拴哥，你有骨头！不怕我这铁筋洋灰的胳臂！

王大拴　你就是把我打死，我不服你还是不服你，不是吗？

小二德子　喝，这么绕脖子的话，你怎么想出来的？大拴哥，你应当去教党义，你有文才！好啦，反正今天我不再打学生！

王大拴　干吗光是今天不打？永远不打才对！

小二德子　不是今天我另有差事吗？

王大拴　什么差事？

小二德子　今天打教员！

王大拴　干吗打教员？打学生就不对，还打教员？

小二德子　上边怎么交派，我怎么干！他们说，教员要罢课。罢课就是不老实，不老实就得揍！他们叫我上这儿等着，

Notes

① nuts /nʌts/ *a.* 发狂的，疯的

② dean /diːn/ *n.* 系主任

③ shooter /ˈʃuːtə/ *n.* 枪炮

④ queer /kwiə/ *a.* 奇怪的，不舒服的

⑤ quit /kwit/ *v.* 离开，停止

⑥ on strike 罢工中

Erdez Jr I go for the easy ones. Think I'm **nuts**[1]?

Wang Dashuan Listen, Erdez Jr, beating up people's wrong.

Erdez Jr Who says so? Look at the **dean**[2] of the institute. He teaches KMT Party doctrines. When he gives a lecture first thing he does is to take out his **shooter**[3] and bang it on the table. Me, I only use my fists, not shooters!

Wang Dashuan Dean indeed! He's a gangster!

Erdez Jr Rig! A gangster! Ah, no, that makes me a gangster too! Now, Brother Dashuan, you've a **queer**[4] way of knocking me! You've got guts! Don't my reinforced concrete muscles scare you?

Wang Dashuan You can beat me to death, but if I never give in, you don't win, do you?

Erdez Jr Such a queer way of saying things! You should come and teach Party doctrines. You've got what it takes. Well, today I won't be beating up any more students.

Wang Dashuan Why only today? **Quit**[5] it altogether.

Erdez Jr I've got another job today.

Wang Dashuan What's that?

Erdez Jr The teachers! I'm going to lick into them!

Wang Dashuan Why? Beating up students is bad enough. Now you want to start on the teachers?

Erdez Jr I do what I'm told. My boss told me the teachers are going **on strike**[6]. That means they're breaking the law. That means they gets what's

看见教员就揍!

邹福远 (嗅出危险)师弟，咱们走吧!

卫福喜 走! (同邹福远下)

小二德子 大拴哥，你拿着这钱吧!

王大拴 打女学生的钱，我不要!

小二德子 (另拿一块)换换，这块是打男学生的，行了吧? (看王大拴还是摇头)这么办，你替我看着点，我出去买点好吃的，请请你，活着还不为吃点喝点老三点吗? (收起现洋，下)

〔康顺子提着小包出来。王利发与周秀花跟着。

康顺子 王掌柜，你要是改了主意，不让我走，我还可以不走!

王利发 我……

周秀花 庞四奶奶也未必敢砸茶馆!

王利发 你怎么知道? 三皇道是好惹的?

康顺子 我顶不放心的还是大力的事! 只要一走漏了消息，大家全完! 那比砸茶馆更厉害!

王大拴 大婶，走! 我送您去! 爸爸，我送送她老人家，可以吧?

① thumping /ˈθʌmpiŋ/ *n.* 敲击，打击

② bloke /bləuk/ *n.* (俚)人，家伙

③ nosh-up *n.* 盛筵，美餐

④ chow /tʃau/ *n.* 食物

⑤ tangle with 与……争吵(或打架)，与……有纠葛

⑥ see sb. off 给……送行

coming to them — a **thumping**①. I was told to wait here and beat up all the teachers I see.

Zou Fuyuan 〔*sensing danger*〕Brother, let's move.

Wei Fuxi Let's. 〔*Exeunt Wei and Zou.*〕

Erdez Jr Here, Brother Dashuan, take this dollar!

Wang Dashuan I won't take money you got for beating up girls.

Erdez Jr 〔*takes out another dollar*〕Then take this one! I got it for beating up the **blokes**②! That's OK, isn't it? 〔*Wang Dashuan still shakes his head.*〕I know what. You keep an eye open for me, and I'll run out and treat you to a good **nosh-up**③! What's life for without good **chow**④, good drinks and a bit of fun? 〔*Pockets the money and goes off.*〕

〔*Kang Shunz comes on carrying a parcel. Wang Lifa and Zhou Xiuhua follow her.*〕

Kang Shunz Manager Wang, if you've changed your mind and want me to stay, I will.

Wang Lifa I —

Zhou Xiuhua Madame Pang won't dare smash up our teahouse.

Wang Lifa How do you know? It doesn't pay to **tangle with**⑤ the "Tri-emperor" Society.

Kang Shunz What really worries me is Dali's coming here last nig. If that leaks out, we're all finished. That's more serious than smashing up the teahouse.

Wang Dashuan Better you leave, aunt! I'll **see you off**⑥. Dad, I can see her off, can't I?

王利发　嗯——

周秀花　大婶在这儿受了多少年的苦，帮了咱们多少忙，还不应当送送？

王利发　我并没说不叫他送！送！送！

王大拴　大婶，等等，我拿件衣服去！（下）

周秀花　爸，您怎么啦？

王利发　别再问我什么，我心里乱！一辈子没这么乱过！媳妇，你先陪大婶走，我叫老大追你们！大婶，外边不行啊，就还回来！

周秀花　老太太，这儿永远是您的家！

王利发　可谁知道也许……

康顺子　我也不会忘了你们！老掌柜，你硬硬朗朗的吧！（同周秀花下）

王利发　（送了两步，立住）硬硬朗朗的干什么呢？

〔谢勇仁和于厚斋进来。

谢勇仁　（看看墙上，先把茶钱放在桌上）老人家，沏一壶来。（坐）

王利发　（先收钱）好吧。

于厚斋　勇仁，这恐怕是咱们末一次坐茶馆了吧？

谢勇仁　以后我倒许常来。我决定改行，去蹬三轮儿！

① muddled /ˈmʌdld/ *a.* 混乱的，乱七八糟的

② throw up 辞掉

Wang Lifa Well —

Zhou Xiuhua All these years aunt has done so much for us. The least we can do is see her off.

Wang Lifa Did I say no? Go ahead, see her off!

Wang Dashuan Just a minute, aunt. I'll fetch a coat.〔*Exit.*〕

Zhou Xiuhua What's up, dad?

Wang Lifa Don't ask me any more questions. Can't think straig. I'm all **muddled**①. Never been so muddled before. Xiuhua, you go with aunt first. I'll tell Dashuan to catch you up. Aunt, if you have any trouble, you just come back!

Zhou Xiuhua This will always be your home, aunt.

Wang Lifa But who knows what will...

Kang Shunz And I'll never forget you. Old manager, I wish you good health yourself! 〔*Goes off with Zhou Xiuhua.*〕

Wang Lifa 〔*follows them a few steps and stops*〕 Good health! What's the use?

〔*Two teachers, Xie Yongren and Yu Houzhai, enter.*〕

Xie Yongren 〔*after a look at the wall, places money on the table*〕 Old manager, a pot of tea, please.〔*Sits.*〕

Wang Lifa 〔*takes money first*〕 Rig.

Yu Houzhai Yongrenn, perhaps this is our last time in a teahouse?

Xie Yongren I may be coming a lot from now on. I've decided to **throw up** ② teaching. I'm going to start

于厚斋 蹬三轮一定比当小学教员强!

谢勇仁 我偏偏教体育，我饿，学生们饿，还要运动，不是笑话吗?

〔王小花跑进来。

王利发 小花，怎这么早就下了学呢?

王小花 老师们罢课啦!（看见于厚斋、谢勇仁）于老师，谢老师!你们都没上学去，不教我们啦?还教我们吧!见不着老师，同学们都哭啦!我们开了个会，商量好，以后一定都守规矩，不招老师们生气!

于厚斋 小花!老师们也不愿意耽误了你们的功课。可是，吃不上饭，怎么教书呢?我们家里也有孩子，为教别人的孩子，叫自己的孩子挨饿，不是不公道吗?好孩子，别着急，喝完茶，我们开会去，也许能够想出点办法来!

谢勇仁 好好在家温书，别乱跑去，小花!

〔王大拴由后面出来，夹着个小包。

王小花 爸，这是我的两位老师!

王大拴 老师们，快走!他们埋伏下了打手!

① pedal /'pedl/ *v.* 用脚踏动，踩踏板

② pedicab /'pedikæb/ *n.* 三轮车

③ upset /ʌp'set/ *v.* 颠覆，扰乱

pedalling[1] a **pedicab**[2] instead!

Yu Houzhai You'll certainly earn more than a primary school teacher!

Xie Yongren It's crazy! Being a gym teacher when both the kids and I are starving!

〔*Wang Xiaohua runs in.*〕

Wang Lifa Why are you back from school so early, Xiaohua?

Wang Xiaohua Our teachers are on strike! 〔*Sees Yu Houzhai and Xie Yongrenn.*〕 Oh, Teacher Yu, Teacher Xie! you weren't at school today. Aren't you going to teach us any more? Oh, please come back! We missed you so much. We were all crying. We had a meeting. Everyone promises to behave and never make you angry again.

Yu Houzhai We hate **upsetting**[3] your studies as much as you do. But we can't teach on empty stomachs. We've children of our own. It isn't fair to let them starve while we teach other children, is it? There, there, don't worry! After we've had our tea, we're going to a meeting. Maybe we can find a way out.

Xie Yongren Stay at home and revise your lessons. Don't go fooling around, Xiaohua.

〔*Wang Dashuan enters from the rear, a parcel under his arm.*〕

Wang Xiaohua Dad, these are my teachers.

Wang Dashuan Teachers! You'd better go away quickly!

王利发　谁?

王大拴　小二德子！他刚出去，就回来！

王利发　二位先生，茶钱退回，（递钱）请吧！快！

王大拴　随我来！

〔小二德子上。

小二德子　街上有游行的，他妈的什么也买不着！大拴哥，你上哪儿？这俩是谁?

王大拴　喝茶的！（同于厚斋、谢勇仁往外走）

小二德子　站住！（三人还走）怎么？不听话？先揍了再说!

王利发　小二德子!

小二德子　(拳已出去）尝尝这个!

谢勇仁　(上面一个嘴巴下面一脚）尝尝这个!

小二德子　哎哟！（倒下）

王小花　该！该!

谢勇仁　起来，再打!

小二德子　(起来，捂着脸）喝！喝！（往后退）喝!

王大拴　快走！（扯二人下）

小二德子　(迁怒）老掌柜，你等着吧，你放走了他们，待会儿我跟你算账！打不

① demonstrator /'demənstreitə/ *n.* 示威者

② round /raund/ *n.* 一回合，一场

③ struggle to one's feet (挣扎着）站起来

④ beat it 跑掉，走开，溜走

They've got a thug lying in wait.

Wang Lifa　Who?

Wang Dashuan　Erdez Jr! He was here a moment ago. He'll be back any time.

Wang Lifa　Gentlemen, here's your money back. 〔*Handing over the money*〕 Please go! Now!

Wang Dashuan　Come with me.

〔*Erdez Jr enters.*〕

Erdez Jr　The streets are full of **demonstrators**①! Can't buy a damn thing! Brother Dashuan, where're you going? Who are those two?

Wang Dashuan　Customers. 〔*On the way out with Yu Houzhai and Xie Yongrenn.*〕

Erdez Jr　Hey! Stop! 〔*The three ignore him.*〕 What's this? Don't listen, eh? I'll show you!

Wang Lifa　Edrez Jr!

Erdez Jr　〔*already swinging his fist*〕 Take this!

Xie Yongren　〔*giving Erdez Jr a slap with his hand and a kick with his foot*〕 And you take this!

Erdez Jr　Ouch! 〔*Falls down.*〕

Wang Xiaohua　Serves you rig! Serves you rig!

Xie Yongren　On your feet! Another **round**②!

Erdez Jr　〔***struggles to his feet***③*, a hand to his face*〕Ow! Ow! 〔*Backing away*〕 Ouch!

Wang Dashuan　Let's **beat it**④! 〔*Drags the two away. Exeunt.*〕

Erdez Jr　〔*venting his anger on Wang Lifa*〕 You just wait, you old fool! You let them get away. You'll pay

了他们，还打不了你这个糟老头子吗？(下)

王小花　爷爷，爷爷！小二德子追老师们去了吧？那可怎么好！

王利发　他不敢！这路人我见多了，都是软的欺，硬的怕！

王小花　他要是回来打您呢？

王利发　我？爷爷会说好话呀。

王小花　爸爸干什么去了？

王利发　出去一会儿，你甭管！上后边温书去吧，乖！

王小花　老师们可别吃了亏呀，我真不放心！(下)

〔丁宝跑进来。

丁　宝　老掌柜，老掌柜！告诉你点事！

王利发　说吧，姑娘！

丁　宝　小刘麻子呀，没安着好心，他要霸占这个茶馆！

王利发　怎么霸占？这个破茶馆还值得他们霸占？

丁　宝　待会儿他们就来，我没工夫细说，你打个主意吧！

王利发　姑娘，我谢谢你！

① duffer /'dʌfə/ *n.* 不中用的东西，糊涂人

② up to no good 不怀好意

③ tip off 事先给的警告(或暗示)

for that! Maybe I can't lick them two, but I can sure beat the shit out of an old **duffer** ① like you! 〔*Exit.*〕

Wang Xiaohua Grandad! Grandad! Is Erdez Jr after our teachers? What can we do?

Wang Lifa Don't worry! He won't dare do anything! I've seen lots like him in my time. Bullies like him are all cowards!

Wang Xiaohua But what if he comes back here after you?

Wang Lifa Me? Grandad knows how to charm him witha few nice words.

Wang Xiaohua Where's dad gone?

Wang Lifa He'll be back soon. Don't worry. Now go and do your lessons. There's a good girl!

Wang Xiaohua I hope nothing will happen to our teachers. I'm so worried! 〔*Exit.*〕

〔*Ding Bao runs in.*〕

Ding Bao Old manager, old manager! I've something to tell you!

Wang Lifa What, miss?

Ding Bao Pock-mark Liu Jr's **up to no good**②. He's going to take over your teahouse!

Wang Lifa How come? What would he want with a shabby old place like this?

Ding Bao They'll be here any moment. No time to explain! You'd better think of something quick!

Wang Lifa Thanks for the **tip off**③, miss.

丁　宝　我好心好意来告诉你，你可不能卖了我呀!

王利发　姑娘，我还没老胡涂了! 放心吧!

丁　宝　好! 待会儿见! （下）

〔周秀花回来。

周秀花　爸，他们走啦。

王利发　好!

周秀花　小花的爸说，叫您放心，他送到了地方就回来。

王利发　回来不回来都随他的便吧!

周秀花　爸，您怎么啦? 干吗这么不高兴?

王利发　没事! 没事! 看小花去吧。她不是想吃热汤面吗? 要是还有点面的话，给她做一碗吧，孩子怪可怜的，什么也吃不着!

周秀花　一点白面也没有! 我看看去，给她做点杂和面儿疙瘩汤吧! （下）

〔小唐铁嘴回来。

小唐铁嘴　王掌柜，说好了吗?

王利发　晚上，晚上一定给你回话!

小唐铁嘴　王掌柜，你说我爸爸白喝了一辈子的茶，我送你几句救命的话，算是替他还账吧。告诉你，三皇道现在比日本人在这儿的时候更厉害，砸你的茶馆比砸个砂锅还容易! 你别

Notes

① tell on sb. 告密，打小报告

② dough /dəu/ *n.* 生面团，浆糊

③ save one's neck 免受绞刑，免于遭殃

Ding Bao I just want to help you! Don't **tell on me**[①]!

Wang Lifa I'm not gaga yet, my girl! Don't worry!

Ding Bao OK. See you later. 〔*Exit.*〕

〔*Zhou Xiuhua comes back.*〕

Zhou Xiuhua Dad, they've gone.

Wang Lifa Good.

Zhou Xiuhua Dashuan said you're not to worry. He'll be back as soon as he's seen her safely there.

Wang Lifa That's up to him!

Zhou Xiuhua Why? What's the matter, dad? Why are you so upset?

Wang Lifa Oh, nothing, nothing! Go and see to Xiaohua. Didn't she want some hot noodles? If there's any flour left, make her some. Poor child, nothing good for her to eat!

Zhou Xiuhua There's not a scrap of flour left in the house! I'll see what I can do. Maybe make a bowl of **dough**[②] drop soup with maize flour. 〔*Exit.*〕

〔*Tang the Oracle Jr returns.*〕

Tang the oracle jr Manager Wang, did you persuade her?

Wang Lifa This evening. I promised you an answer this evening.

Tang the oracle jr You were complaining my father never paid you for his tea. So, in return, here's a piece of advice which may **save your neck**[③]. Listen, the "Tri-emperor" Society's even stronger now than under the Japs. Smashing up a teahouse

太大意了！

王利发 我知道！你既买我的好，又好去对娘娘表表功！是吧？

〔小宋恩子和小吴祥子进来，都穿着新洋服。

小唐铁嘴 二位，今天可够忙的？

小宋恩子 忙得厉害！教员们大暴动！

王利发 二位，“罢课”改了名儿，叫“暴动”啦？

小唐铁嘴 怎么啦？

小吴祥子 他们还能反到天上去吗？到现在为止，已经抓了一百多，打了七十几个，叫他们反吧！

小宋恩子 太不知好歹！他们老老实实的，美国会送来大米、白面嘛！

小唐铁嘴 就是！二位，有大米、白面，可别忘了我！以后，给大家的坟地看风水，我一定尽义务！好！二位忙吧！(下)

小吴祥子 你刚才问，“罢课”改叫“暴动”啦？王掌柜！

① get one's back up 惹某人生气，把某人给惹翻了

② get in one's good books 得到某人的好感（或赞许）

③ beat the daylights out of 吓得……失去知觉

④ toe the line 服从，听从

⑤ divine /di'vain/ *v.* 占卜，预测

like yours is kidsplay to them! You'd better watch out!

Wang Lifa Oh, I understand alrig! You don't want to **get my back up**[①]. Yet at the same time you want to **get in your empress' good books**[②]. Rig?

〔*Song Enz Jr and Wu Xiangz Jr enter, both in brand-new western-style suits.*〕

Tang the oracle jr Gentlemen, quite a busy day, eh?

Song Enz jr Too damn busy! There's a teachers' riot!

Wang Lifa So, now you gentlemen call it a "riot" instead of a "strike"?

Tang the oracle jr What's happening?

Wu Xiangz jr They won't get away with it! We've already nabbed more than a hundred and **beat the dayligs out of**[③] more than seventy. That'll teach them!

Song Enz jr They don't know on which side their bread's buttered. If they **toe the line**[④], the Yankees will send over rice and flour.

Tang the oracle jr Exactly. If there's any rice and flour on the way, don't forget me! When the time comes to **divine**[⑤] an auspicious site for your ancestral tombs, I'll do it for free. Well, gentlemen, back to business! 〔*Exit.*〕

Wu Xiangz jr You were asking just now, how a "strike" becomes a "riot", weren't you, Manager Wang?

王利发　岁数大了，不懂新事，问问!

小宋恩子　哼! 你就跟他们是一路货!

王利发　我? 您太高抬我啦!

小吴祥子　我们忙，没工夫跟你费话，说干脆的吧!

王利发　什么干脆的?

小宋恩子　教员们暴动，必有主使的人!

王利发　谁?

小吴祥子　昨天晚上谁上这儿来啦?

王利发　康大力!

小宋恩子　就是他! 你把他交出来吧!

王利发　我要是知道他是哪路人，还能够随便说出来吗? 我跟你们的爸爸打交道多少年，还不懂这点道理?

小吴祥子　甭跟我们拍老腔，说真的吧!

王利发　交人，还是拿钱，对吧?

小宋恩子　你真是我爸爸教出来的! 对啦，要是不交人，就把你的金条拿出来! 别的铺子都随开随倒，你可混了这么多年，必定有点底!

〔小二德子匆匆跑来。

小二德子　快走! 街上的人不够用啦! 快走!

小吴祥子　你小子管干吗的?

小二德子　我没闲着，看，脸都肿啦!

① fangle /'fæŋgəl/ *v.* 发明（新款式）

② brass tacks 基本事实

③ stash away 藏起，隐藏

Wang Lifa I'm too old to understand new-**fangled**① things. I just asked, that's all.

Song Enz jr H'm! You all belong to the same bunch.

Wang Lifa Me? You flatter me!

Wu Xiangz jr We got no time to waste on you. Let's make it snappy.

Wang Lifa That means?

Song Enz jr There's someone behind the teachers' riot.

Wang Lifa Who?

Wu Xiangz jr Who came here last nig?

Wang Lifa Kang Dali!

Song Enz jr That's the man! Hand him over!

Wang Lifa If I'd known he was such a character, would I have told you his name? I dealt with your fathers long enough to learn at least that much, I hope!

Wu Xiangz jr Talking about your age won't get you anywhere! Let's get down to **brass tacks**②.

Wang Lifa Hand him over or else pay up! Rig?

Song Enz jr Dad trained you well! You said it yourself! Either hand him over or those gold bars you've **stashed away**③. Other shops come and go, but you've managed to keep your head above water. You must have a neat little pile tucked away somewhere.

〔*Erdez Jr rushes in.*〕

Erdez Jr Come quick! There ain't enough of us in the streets. Hurry up!

Wu Xiangz jr You little bastard, what are you paid for?

Erdez Jr I fuckin' did my best. Take a look at my face!

小宋恩子　掌柜的，我们马上回来，你打主意吧!

王利发　不怕我跑了吗?

小吴祥子　老梆子，你真逗气儿!你跑到阴间去，我们也会把你抓回来!（打了王利发一掌，同小宋恩子、小二德子下）

王利发　（向后叫）小花!小花的妈!

周秀花　（同王小花跑出来）我都听见了!怎么办?

王利发　快走!追上康妈妈!快!

王小花　我拿书包去!（下）

周秀花　拿上两件衣裳，小花!爸，剩您一个人怎么办?

王利发　这是我的茶馆，我活在这儿，死在这儿!

〔王小花挎着书包，夹着点东西跑回来。

周秀花　爸爸!

王小花　爷爷!

王利发　都别难过，走!（从怀中掏出所有的钱和一张旧像片）媳妇，拿着这点钱!小花，拿着这个，老裕泰三十年前的像片，交给你爸爸!走吧!

〔小刘麻子同丁宝回来。

① swollen /'swəulən/ *a.* 肿大的，水涨的

② jiffy /'dʒifi/ *n.* 瞬间，一会儿

③ satchel /'sætʃəl/ *n.* （皮或帆布的）书包

④ sling /sliŋ/ *v.* 用吊钩钓上

It's all **swollen**[1]!

Song Enz jr Manager, we'll be back in a **jiffy**[2]. So make up your mind.

Wang Lifa You aren't afraid I'll run off?

Wu Xiangz jr Giving us some of your lip, are you, you old devil? We'll follow you to hell even! 〔*Slaps Wang Lifa, then goes off with Song Enz Jr and Erdez Jr.*〕

Wang Lifa 〔*calling to the rear*〕 Xiaohua! Dauger-in-law!

Zhou Xiuhua 〔*rushing out with Wang Xiaohua*〕 I heard everything! What are we going to do?

Wang Lifa Get out of here! Try to catch up with Aunt Kang! At once!

Wang Xiaohua I'll get my **satchel**[3]. 〔*Exit.*〕

Zhou Xiuhua Take some clothes along, Xiaohua. Dad, what will you do all alone?

Wang Lifa This is my teahouse. I've lived in it. I'll die in it! 〔*Wang Xiaohua, her schoolbag* **slung**[4] *over her shoulder and some things under her arm, runs back.*〕

Zhou Xiuhua Dad!

Wang Xiaohua Grandad!

Wang Lifa Don't cry! Off you go now! 〔*Takes out all his money and an old photograph.*〕 Dauger-in-law, take the money. Xiaohua, you take this. It's a photo of the old Yutai Teahouse taken thirty years ago. Give it to your dad. Now go! 〔*Pock-mark Liu Jr and Ding Bao come back.*〕

小刘麻子	小花，教员罢课，你住姥姥家去呀？
王小花	对啦！
王利发	（假意地）媳妇，早点回来！
周秀花	爸，我们住两天就回来！（同王小花下）
小刘麻子	王掌柜，好消息！沈处长批准了我的计划！
王利发	大喜，大喜！
小刘麻子	您也大喜，处长也批准修理这个茶馆！我一说，处长说好！他呀老把“好”说成“蒿”，特别有个洋味儿！
王利发	都是怎么一回事？
小刘麻子	从此你算省心了！这儿全属我管啦，你搬出去！我先跟你说好了，省得以后你麻烦我！
王利发	那不能！凑巧，我正想搬家呢。
丁　宝	小刘，老掌柜在这儿多少年啦，你就不照顾他一点吗？
小刘麻子	看吧！我办事永远厚道！王掌柜，我接处长去，叫他看看这个地方。你把这儿好好收拾一下！小丁宝，你把小心眼找来，迎接处长！带点香水，好好喷一气，这里臭哄哄的！走！（同丁宝下）

① cue /kjuː/ *n.* 提词，暗示

② pester /ˈpestə/ *v.* 使烦恼，使苦恼

③ coincidence /kəuˈinsidəns/ *n.* 巧合

④ spray /sprei/ *v.* 喷雾，喷射

Pock-markliu jr Xiaohua, going to your granny's because the teachers are on strike?

Wang Xiaohua Yes.

Wang Lifa 〔*taking up the* **cue**[1]〕 Xiuhua, be back soon!

Zhou Xiuhua Dad, We'll only stay a couple of days. 〔*Goes off with Xiaohua.*〕

Pock-markliu jr Wonderful news, Manager Wang. Director Shen's approved my plan.

Wang Lifa Congratulations!

Pock-markliu jr Congratulations to you too! The director also approved fixing up the teahouse. As soon as I suggested it he said "Okay". It's the way he says it: "Okay! " Just like a foreigner!

Wang Lifa What's all this about?

Pock-markliu jr Your troubles are over! The whole place will be managed by me. You can clear out. Get this straig now. I don't want you **pestering**[2] me later on.

Wang Lifa Don't worry! Pure **coincidence**[3]! I'm on the point of moving out myself.

Ding Bao Pock-mark, the old manager's been here for ages. That's no way to treat him.

Pock-markliu jr We'll see. I always play fair. Now, Manager Wang, I'm going to fetch the director to look over this place. You tidy it up! Baby, you get hold of Xiao Xinyar. The two of you should be here to welcome the director. Remember to bring some perfume and **spray**[4] it around the place. It

王利发 好！真好！太好！哈哈哈！

〔常四爷提着小筐进来，筐里有些纸钱和花生米。他虽年过七十，可是腰板还不太弯。

常四爷 什么事这么好哇，老朋友！

王利发 哎哟！常四哥！我正想找你这么一个人说说话儿呢！我沏一壶顶好的茶来，咱们喝喝！（去沏茶）

〔秦仲义进来。他老的不像样子了，衣服也破旧不堪。

秦仲义 王掌柜在吗？

常四爷 在！您是……

秦仲义 我姓秦。

常四爷 秦二爷！

王利发 （端茶来）谁？秦二爷？正想去告诉您一声，这儿要大改良！坐！坐！

常四爷 我这儿有点花生米，（抓）喝茶吃花生米，这可真是个乐子！

秦仲义 可是谁嚼得动呢？

王利发 看多么邪门，好容易有了花生米，可全嚼不动！多么可笑！怎样啊？秦二

Notes

① stink /stiŋk/ *v.* 发臭味

② scatter /'skætə/ *v.* 散开，散播

③ chew /tʃuː/ *v.* 咀嚼，嚼碎

stinks[1]. Let's go! 〔*Goes off with Ding Bao.*〕

Wang Lifa Wonderful! Truly wonderful! Too wonderful to be true! Ha! Ha!

〔*Master Chang enters with a small basket, in which there are some peanuts and paper money — white paper cut in the shape of coins which is* **scattered**[2] *at funerals for the dead to use in the next life. He's over seventy but still holds himself straig.*〕

Chang What's so wonderful, my old friend?

Wang Lifa Why, Brother Chang! Just the man I was wanting to have a chat with. I'll make a pot of the very best tea. We'll drink it together. 〔*Goes off to make the tea.*〕

〔*Qin Zhongyi enters. He has aged beyond recognition and is very shabbily dressed.*〕

Qin Zhongyi Is Manager Wang here?

Chang Yes he is. You're —?

Qin Zhongyi My name's Qin.

Chang Master Qin!

Wang Lifa 〔*bringing the tea*〕 Who? Master Qin? I was just thinking of telling you, another great "reform" is about to take place. Sit down! Sit down!

Chang I've got some peanuts here. 〔*Taking some out with his hand*〕 Tea and peanuts, what more can you want?

Qin Zhongyi But who's going to **chew**[3] them?

Wang Lifa Well, I never! At last we manage to get hold of some peanuts but we've no teeth left to chew them

Notes

爷！（都坐下）

秦仲义 别人都不理我啦，我来跟你说说：我到天津去了一趟，看看我的工厂！

王利发 不是没收了吗？又物归原主啦？这可是喜事！

秦仲义 拆了！

常四爷
王利发 拆了？

秦仲义 拆了！我四十年的心血啊，拆了！别人不知道，王掌柜你知道：我从二十多岁起，就主张实业救国。到而今……抢去我的工厂，好，我的势力小，干不过他们！可倒好好地办哪，那是富国裕民的事业呀！结果，拆了，机器都当碎铜烂铁卖了！全世界，全世界找得到这样的政府找不到？我问你！

① advocate /'ædvəkit/ *v.* 主张，提倡
② salvation /sæl'veiʃən/ *n.* 得救，拯救
③ prosper /'prɔspə/ *v.* 兴隆，成功
④ demolish /di'mɔliʃ/ *v.* 毁，破坏

王利发 当初，我开的好好的公寓，您非盖仓库不可。看，仓库查封，货物全叫他们偷光！当初，我劝您别把财产都出手，您非都卖了开工厂不可！

⑤ warehouse /'wɛəhaus/ *n.* 仓库
⑥ seal /siːl/ *v.* 盖印，封闭

with! Isn't that a joke? How are things with you, Master Qin? [*They sit down.*]

Qin Zhongyi No one wants to listen to me any more, so I've come to you. I just went to Tianjin to have a look at my factory.

Wang Lifa But it was confiscated, wasn't it? So they've given it back to its rigul owner again? Congratulations!

Qin Zhongyi It's been pulled down!

Chang
Wang Lifa Pulled down?

Qin Zhongyi Flattened! Forty years of my sweat and blood razed to the ground! Others may not know it but you do, Manager Wang. From my twenties I **advocated**① national **salvation**② through industry. And now... when they seized my factory, I couldn't lift a finger. I was a nobody. No match for them! Still I hoped they'd run it well. It could have helped the country to **prosper**③ and benefited the people. Now **demolished**④! All the machines sold as scrap! Where in the world, in the whole wide world, can you find a government like this one? I ask you!

Wang Lifa Years ago, my boarding-house was doing fine. But you insisted on building your **warehouse**⑤ here. Then what happened? The warehouse was **sealed**⑥ up and all the goods stolen! Years ago, I warned you not to sell off all your property. But you insisted so you could start your factory!

常四爷 还记得吧？当初，我给那个卖小妞的小媳妇一碗面吃，您还说风凉话呢。

秦仲义 现在我明白了！王掌柜，求你一件事吧：（掏出一二机器小零件和一支钢笔管来）工厂拆平了，这是我由那儿捡来的小东西。这支笔上刻着我的名字呢，它知道，我用它签过多少张支票，写过多少计划书。我把它们交给你，没事的时候，你可以跟喝茶的人们当个笑话谈谈，你说呀：当初有那么一个不知好歹的秦某人，爱办实业。办了几十年，临完他只由工厂的土堆里捡回来这么点小东西！你应当劝告大家，有钱哪，就该吃喝嫖赌，故作非为，可千万别干好事！告诉他们哪，秦某人七十多岁了才明白这点大道理！他是天生来的笨蛋！

王利发 您自己拿着这支笔吧，我马上就搬家啦！

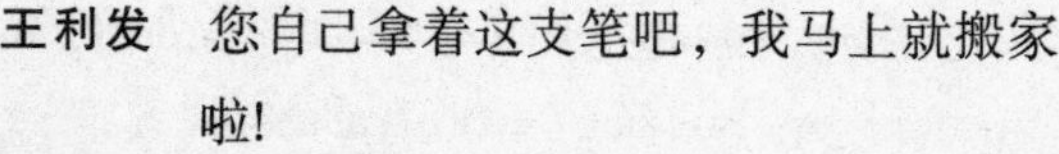

常四爷 搬到哪儿去？

王利发 哪儿不一样呢！秦二爷，常四爷，我跟你们不一样：二爷财大业大心胸大，树大可就招风啊！四爷你，一辈子不服

Notes

① mock /mɔk/ *v.* 嘲弄，轻视

② rubble /ˈrʌbl/ *n.* 粗石，破碎的砖

③ engrave /inˈgreiv/ *v.* 雕刻

④ draw up 拟定，起草

⑤ salvage /ˈsælvidʒ/ *v.* 救捞，废物利用

⑥ moral /ˈmɔrəl/ *n.* 寓意

Chang Remember when? The time I gave that young woman selling her dauger two bowls of noodles and you **mocked**[①] me.

Qin Zhongyi Well, I know better now! Manager Wang, I want to ask you a favour. 〔*Takes out one or two small machine parts and a pen-holder.*〕 My factory's been razed to the ground. This is all I picked up from the **rubble**[②]. This pen-holder has my name **engraved**[③] on it. A witness to the number of cheques I signed and the number of plans I **drew up**[④]. I'll leave these things with you. You can tell your customers stories about them when you've nothing better to do. Tell them, once upon a time there was a foolish man called Qin who was mad on industrialization. After many years, these were the only things he **salvaged**[⑤] from the rubble of his factory. The **moral**[⑥] of this story is, if you have money spend it all on wine, women and gambling. Only enjoy life. Never try to do anything useful! Tell them, this man called Qin didn't understand these simple truths until he was in his seventies, because he was a real bloody fool!

Wang Lifa You'd better take care of the pen-holder yourself. I'm moving out of here soon.

Chang Where to?

Wang Lifa What does that matter? Master Qin, Master Chang, I'm not as great as you. Master Qin, you had a great wealth and ambitions. But, as they say, it's the tall

软，敢作敢当，专打抱不平。我呢，做了一辈子顺民，见谁都请安、鞠躬、作揖。我只盼着呀，孩子们有出息，冻不着，饿不着，没灾没病！可是，日本人在这儿，二拴子逃跑啦，老婆想儿子想死啦！好容易，日本人走啦，该缓一口气了吧？谁知道，（惨笑）哈哈，哈哈，哈哈！

常四爷 我也不比你强啊！自食其力，凭良心干了一辈子啊，我一事无成！七十多了，只落得卖花生米！个人算什么呢，我盼哪，盼哪，只盼国家像个样儿，不受外国人欺侮。可是……哈哈！

秦仲义 日本人在这儿，说什么合作，把我的工厂就合作过去了。咱们的政府回来了，工厂也不怎么又变成了逆产。仓库里（指后边）有多少货呀，全完！哈哈！

王利发 改良，我老没忘了改良，总不肯落在人家后头。卖茶不行啊，开公寓。公寓没啦，添评书！评书也不叫座儿呀，

Notes

① brunt /brʌnt/ *n.* 正面的冲击，主要的压力

② obedient /ə'biːdjənt/ *a.* 服从的，顺从的

③ scrap /skræp/ *n.* 少量，点滴，片断

④ grotesquely /grəu'teskli/ *ad.* 奇异地，荒诞地

⑤ lag /læg/ *v.* 落后

⑥ pack up 停止工作，出故障

tree that bears the **brunt**[1] of the storm. And you, Master Chang, you never gave in, never accepted injustice to yourself or to others. You never feared the consequences. Me, I've been an **obedient**[2] subject all my life. I bowed and **scraped**[3] to everyone. I only wanted a good future for my children. Food and clothes. To be safe and sound. Then, when the Japs were here, my second son ran off. My old missus died of a broken heart and worry. When the Japs finally left, we all hoped life would be better. Who'd have thoug — 〔*Laughs* ***grotesquely***[4].〕 Ha! Ha! ...

Chang I'm no better off than you! I earned my own living and worked hard all my life. But where's that got me? Selling peanuts in my seventies. One man's life doesn't count. But what I hoped for was that our country would become a decent place. No longer sat on by foreign powers. But —Ha! Ha! ...

Qin Zhongyi When the Japs were here, they called it coopera-tion. That was the last I saw of my factory. When our own government came back, my factory somehow became traitor's property. All the goods in the warehouse 〔*pointing to the rear*〕 were taken away! Ha! Ha! ...

Wang Lifa Reform, that's one thing I never forgot! Always afraid I'd **lag**[5] behind. When tea wasn't selling well, I started the boarding-house. When that **packed up**[6],

好，不怕丢人，想添女招待！人总得活着吧？我变尽了方法，不过是为活下去！是呀，该贿赂的，我就递包袱。我可没做过缺德的事，伤天害理的事，为什么就不叫我活着呢？我得罪了谁？谁？皇上，娘娘那些狗男女都活得有滋有味的，单不许我吃窝窝头，谁出的主意？

常四爷 盼哪，盼哪，只盼谁都讲理，谁也不欺侮谁！可是，眼看着老朋友们一个个的不是饿死，就是叫人家杀了，我呀就是有眼泪也流不出来喽！松二爷，我的朋友，饿死啦，连棺材还是我给他化缘化来的！他还有我这么个朋友，给他化了一口四块板的棺材；我自己呢？我爱咱们的国呀，可是谁爱我呢？看（从筐中拿出些纸钱），遇见出殡的，我就捡几张纸钱。没有寿衣，没有棺材，我只好给自己预备下点纸钱吧，哈哈，哈哈！

秦仲义 四爷，让咱们祭奠祭奠自己，把纸钱撒起来，算咱们三个老头子的吧！

王利发 对！四爷，照老年间出殡的规矩，喊

Notes

① draw /drɔː/ *n.* 吸引注意力的人或物

② swallow /'swɔləu/ *v.* 吞下，忍受

③ bribe /braib/ *n.* 贿赂

④ alms /ɑːmz/ *n.* 救济金，救济品

⑤ coffin /'kɔfin/ *n.* 棺材

⑥ fogey /'fəugi/ *n.* 守旧者

I threw in story-telling as a **draw**①. When that didn't work, I **swallowed**② my pride to hire a waitress! One has to live! I did everything just so that we could live! Yes, I handed over **bribes**③ when I had to. But I never did anything bad or criminal. Why shouldn't I be allowed to live? Who have I hurt? Who? All those bastards, that "emperor" and his "empress" are having the time of their lives. Why am I singled out to starve? Whose bloody idea is this?

Chang All I hoped for is that everyone would be fair and no one bullied. But I saw with my own eyes how my friends, one by one, starved to death or were killed off. I wanted to weep, but no tears came! Master Song, my friend, starved to death! I had to go and beg **alms**④ to get a **coffin**⑤ for him. He was lucky to have a friend like me who could get him a rough coffin made of thin planks. What'll happen to me when my time comes? I love our country, but who loves me? See here, 〔*taking out paper money from his basket*〕 whenever I see a funeral, I try to pick up some of this paper money. I won't have any burial clothes. I won't even have a coffin. All I can do isto save some paper money for myself. Ha! Ha! ...

Qin Zhongyi Master Chang, let's offer some sacrifice to ourselves. Throw the paper money in the air. Something special for us three old **fogeys**⑥!

Wang Lifa Rig! Master Chang, don't forget to chant it like in

喊!

常四爷　(立起，喊）四角儿的跟夫，本家赏钱一百二十吊!（撒起几张纸钱）

秦仲义
　　　一百二十吊!
王利发

秦仲义　(一手拉住一个）我没的说了，再见吧!（下）

王利发　再见!

常四爷　再喝你一碗!（一饮而尽）再见!（下)

王利发　再见!

〔丁宝与小心眼进来。

丁　宝　他们来啦，老大爷!（往屋中喷香水)

王利发　好，他们来，我躲开!（捡起纸钱，往后边走)

小心眼　老大爷，干吗撒纸钱呢?

王利发　谁知道!（下)

〔小刘麻子进来。

小刘麻子　来啦! 一边一个站好!

〔丁宝、小心眼分左右在门内立好。

〔门外有汽车停住声，先进来两个宪兵。沈处长进来，穿军便服；高靴，带马刺；手执小鞭。后面跟着二宪

Notes

① pall /pɔːl/ *n.* 棺罩，幕

② gulp /gʌlp/ *n.* 一大口

③ spur /spəː/ *n.* 马刺

the old days!

Chang [*stands up, chanting*] **Pall**[1]-bearers at the four corners, from the family, a reward of one hundred and twenty strings of cash! [*Throws the paper money into the air.*]

Qin Zhongyi
Wang Lifa One hundred and twenty strings of cash!

Qin Zhongyi [*holding a hand of each*] No need to say any more. Goodbye! [*Exit.*]

Wang Lifa Goodbye!

Chang One last cup of yours! [*Drinks it at one* ***gulp***[2].] Goodbye! [*Exit.*]

Wang Lifa Goodbye!

[*Ding Bao and Xiao Xinyar enter.*]

Ding Bao They're here, Mr Wang! [*Spraying perfume in the room.*]

Wang Lifa Good. I'll make room for them. [*Picks up the paper money and heads for the rear.*]

Xiao Xinyar Mr Wang, why the paper money?

Wang Lifa Who knows? [*Exit.*]

[*Pock-mark Liu Jr enters.*]

Pock-markliu jr Here he comes. One on each side, attention!

[*Ding Bao and Xiao Xinyar stand either side of the entrance.*]

[*The sound of a car stopping outside the entrance. Two military policemen enter first. Director Shen enters in off-duty clothes, riding boots and* ***spurs***[3],

兵。

沈处长 (检阅似的，看丁宝、小心眼，看完一个说一声) 好 (蒿)!

〔丁宝摆上一把椅子，请沈处长坐。

小刘麻子 报告处长，老裕泰开了六十多年，九城闻名，地点也好，借着这个老字号，做我们的一个据点，一定成功! 我打算照旧卖茶，派 (指) 小丁宝和小心眼做招待。有我在这儿监视着三教九流，各色人等，一定能够得到大量的情报，捉拿共产党!

沈处长 好 (蒿)!

〔丁宝由宪兵手里接过骆驼牌烟，上前献烟；小心眼接过打火机，点烟。

小刘麻子 后面原来是仓库，货物已由处长都处理了，现在空着。我打算修理一下，中间做小舞厅，两旁布置几间卧室，都带卫生设备。处长清闲的时候，可以来跳跳舞，玩玩牌，喝喝咖啡。天晚了，高兴住下，您就住下。这就算是处长个人的小俱乐

Notes

① inspection /in'spekʃən/ *n.* 检查，视察

② all walks of life 各界人士

③ ballroom /'bɔːlrum/ *n.* 舞厅

with a short whip in his hand. Two more military policemen follow him in.]

SHEN [*as at a military* **inspection**①, *he examines Ding Bao and Xiao Xinyar. After looking at them*] Okay!

[*Ding Bao gets a chair for Shen to sit in.*]

Pock-markliu jr May I report? The old Yutai has been in business for more than sixty years. It's well-known in every part of Beijing. Well-situated too! Such an old name would be ideal for our purposes of setting up an intelligence centre. I carry on selling tea here, and [*pointing*] Little Ding Bao and Xiao Xinyar will be the waitresses. I'll be here keeping an eye on people from **all walks of life**②. We're sure to pick up a lot of information and get our hands on the Commies!

Shen Okay!

[*Ding Bao takes a packet of Camel cigarettes from a policeman and offers one to Shen; Xiao Xinyar takes a liger and ligs it for him.*]

Pock-markliu jr Behind here there used to be a warehouse. You've already got rid of the goods in it. It's quite empty now. I'm going to do it up, with a small **ballroom**③ in the middle and a few bedrooms at the side, complete with bathrooms. When you have a moment to relax, sir, you can come here to dance, play cards and have coffee. If it's late, and

部，由我管理，一定要比公馆里更洒脱一点，方便一点，热闹一点！

沈处长 好（蒿）！

丁　宝 处长，我可以请示一下吗？

沈处长 好（蒿）！

丁　宝 这儿的老掌柜怪可怜的。好不好给他做一身制服，叫他看看门，招呼贵宾们上下汽车？他在这儿几十年了，谁都认识他，简直可以算是老头儿商标！

沈处长 好（蒿）！传！

小刘麻子 是！（往后跑）王掌柜！老掌柜！我爸爸的老朋友，老大爷！（入。过一会儿又跑回来）报告处长，他也不是怎么上了吊，吊死啦！

沈处长好（蒿）！好（蒿）！

—剧　终—

Notes

① residence /'rezidəns/ *n.* 住处，住宅

② trademark /'treidmɑːk/ *n.* 商标

③ summon /'sʌmən/ *v.* 召唤，召集

you feel like it, you can stay the nig. Like it's your private club. With me in charge, compared to your official **residence**①, it'll be easier, freer and gayer!

Shen Okay!

Ding Bao Director, may I make a suggestion?

Shen Okay!

Ding Bao It's a pity about the poor old manager here. If we give him a doorman's uniform, he can take care of the honoured guests getting in and out of cars. He's been here for ages. Everyone knows him. He's like a **trademark**②!

Shen Okay! **Summon**③ him!

Pock-markliu jr Yes, sir! 〔*Runs to the back.*〕 Manager Wang! Ol d manager! Friend of my father! Old Mr Wang! 〔*Disappears. Reappears a moment later.*〕 May I report, sir, he's hanged himself! He's dead!

Shen Okay! Okay!

—END OFPLAY—

附　录

Notes

此剧幕与幕之间须留较长时间，以便人物换装，故拟由一人（也算剧中人）唱几句快板，使休息时间不显着过长，同时也可以略略介绍剧情。

① devise /di'vaiz/ *v.* 设计

② clapper /'klæpə/ *n.* 铃舌，响板

③ entr'acte

④ interval /'intəvəl/ *n.* 间隔

第一幕　幕　前

大傻杨　（我）

大傻杨，打竹板儿，
一来来到大茶馆儿。
大茶馆，老裕泰，
生意兴隆真不赖。
茶座多，真热闹，
也有老来也有少；
有的说，有的唱，

⑤ booming /'buːmiŋ/ *a.* 兴旺的，繁荣的

⑥ brisk /brisk/ *a.* 活跃的，快的

Appendix

As some time must be allowed between the acts for the actors to change their make-up, I have **devised** ① a character (who should be considered as one of the dramatis personae) reciting improvised doggerels with bamboo **clappers**② as a sort of **entr'acte**③. That may make the **intervals**④ seem shorter and at the same time give people some idea about the background of the play.

Act One [*Before the curtain rises*]

Silly Yang [*recites*]

I'm Silly Yang, and from shop to shop,
I make my rounds till here I stop.
This great teahouse, Yutai by name,
A **booming**⑤ business, fortune and fame.
Trade is **brisk**⑥, lots of tea sold,
Everyone welcome, young and old.
Some sing or hum, others sit and chat,

穿着打扮一人一个样；
有提笼，有架鸟，
蛐蛐蝈蝈也都养得好；
有的吃，有的喝，
没有钱的只好白瞧着。
爱下棋，(您）来两盘儿，
赌一卖（碟）干炸丸子外洒胡椒盐儿。
讲排场，讲规矩，
咳嗽一声都像唱大戏。
有一样，听我说：
莫谈国事您得老记着。
哼！国家事（可）不好了，
黄龙旗子一天倒比一天威风小。
文武官，有一宝，
见着洋人赶快跑。
外国货，堆成山，
外带贩卖鸦片烟。
最苦是，乡村里，
没吃没穿逼得卖儿女。
官儿阔，百姓穷，
朝中出了一个谭嗣同，
讲维新，主意高，
还有那康有为和梁启超。
这件事，闹得凶，
气得太后咬牙切齿直哼哼。
她要杀，她要砍，
讲维新的都是要造反。

Notes

① cricket /ˈkrikit/ *n.* 板球，蟋蟀

② grasshopper /ˈgrɑːshɔpə(r)/ *n.* 蚱蜢

③ crumb /krʌm/ *n.* 碎屑，面包心

④ pomp /pɔmp/ *n.* 盛观，夸耀

⑤ turn tail 逃跑，躲开

⑥ plight /plait/ *n.* 困境，苦境

⑦ reverse /riˈvəːs/ *n.* 相反，逆转

⑧ despot /ˈdespɔt/ *n.* 暴君，专制者

⑨ doom /duːm/ *n.* 厄运，毁灭

⑩ presage /ˈpresidʒ/ *v.* 成为……的前兆，预示

⑪ bud /bʌd/ *n.* 芽，花蕾

Each in his gown, each in his hat.
This is where bird fanciers meet,
Where **cricket**[①]-and **grasshopper**[②]-owners compete.
With tea and snacks, you can while away the day,
But not a **crumb**[③] for those who cannot pay.
Here chess players meet for their favourite game,
Tasty meat balls, the winners claim.
Pomp[④] is loved, but manners one must note,
Everything has style, even clearing the throat.
But above all else, get this straig,
Never, if you please, discuss affairs of state.
Matters there, alas, aren't good at all,
The Great Qing Empire seems heading for a fall.
Mandarins and generals have one common trick,
Faced by foreign armies, they **turn tail**[⑤] double quick.
Foreign goods you'll find everywhere,
With opium thrown in as an extra fare.
The peasants' **plight**[⑥], words cannot say,
Forced to sell their children, there's no other way.
The rich got richer, the poor got worse,
Till Tan Sitong demanded a **reverse**[⑦].
Kang Youwei supported him and Liang Qichao,
All wanting the reforms, here and now.
But such changes the **despots'**[⑧] **doom**[⑨] **presaged**[⑩],
No wonder the Empress Dowager was enraged.
"Treason! " she screamed, wanting blood,
So the movement was crushed, nipped in the **bud**[⑪].

这些事，别多说，
说着说着就许掉脑壳。
〔幕徐启。大傻杨入茶馆。

打竹板，迈大步，
走进茶馆找主顾。
哪位爷，愿意听，
《辕门斩子》来了穆桂英。
〔王利发来干涉。
王掌柜，大发财，金银元宝一齐来。
您有钱，我有嘴，数来宝的是穷鬼。
(下)

第二幕　幕　前

大傻杨　打竹板，我又来，
数来宝的还是没发财。
现而今，到民国，
剪了小辫还是没有辙。
王掌柜，动脑筋，
事事改良讲维新。
(低声) 动脑筋，白费力，
胳臂拧不过大腿去。
闹军阀，乱打仗，

① reveal /ri'vi:l/ *v.* 显示，透露

② intervene /ˌintə'vi:n/ *v.* 插入，干涉

③ rhyme /raim/ *n.* 韵，韵文

④ acquiesce /ˌækwi'es/ *v.* 默许，勉强同意

But I'd better stop and hold myself in check,
Talking too freely will surely risk my neck!
〔*The curtain rises* **revealing**① *the teahouse, into which Silly Yang enters.*〕
Beating my clappers, into the teahouse I go,
Hoping that somebody some interest will show.
Would you like a story to cheer you up
Of heroes and heroines, while you enjoy your cup?
〔*Wang Lifa comes over to* **intervene**②.〕
Manager Wang, for you these seem profitable times,
Don't be hard on poor old me, living by my **rhymes**③!
〔*Exit.*〕

Act Two 〔*Before the curtain rises*〕

Silly Yang 〔*recites*〕
Beating my clappers, here I am again,
Life's hard for a rhymester, so a beggar I remain.
The Republic was set up and we all did **acquiesce**④,
Our pigtails were cut off, but the country's still a mess.
Manager Wang, reforming, all the tricks did play,
To give his teahouse a new look in every way.
〔*Sotto voce*〕But all his efforts, alas, are looking pretty thin,
For with heads he lost, nor with tails did win.

白脸的进去黑脸的上，
赵打钱，孙打李，
赵钱孙李乱打一气谁都不讲理。
为打仗，要枪炮，
一堆一堆给洋人老爷送钞票。
为卖炮，为卖枪，
帮助军阀你占黄河他占扬子江。
老百姓，遭了殃，
大兵一到粮食牲口一扫光。
王掌柜，会改良，
茶馆好像大学堂，
后边住，大学生，
说话文明真好听。
就怕呀，兵野蛮，
进来几个茶馆就玩完。
先别说，丧气话，
向他道喜是个好办法。
他开张，我道喜，
编点新词我也了不起。
〔下。
〔又上。

大傻杨 老裕泰，大改良，
万事亨通一天准比一天强。

王利发 今天不打发，明天才开张哪。

大傻杨 明天好，明天妙，

Notes

① rampant /ˈræmpənt/ *a.* 猖獗的，蔓延的

② oust /aust/ *v.* 逐出，夺取

③ carve /kɑːv/ *v.* 切，雕刻

④ sphere /sfiə/ *n.* 范围，领域

⑤ squeeze /skwiːz/ *v.* 紧握，挤压

⑥ zeal /ziːl/ *n.* 热情，热忱

⑦ brutish /ˈbruːtiʃ/ *a.* 野兽般的，野蛮的

⑧ wreck /rek/ *v.* 破坏

⑨ mingle /ˈmiŋgl/ *v.* 混合，联合

Warlords were **rampant**[1], civil wars routine,
One warlord hardly **ousted**[2], another on the scene.
Zhao would fig Qian and Sun would fig Li,
Wars involving thousands for no reason one could see.
In order to fig, one must buy guns,
So to foreign countries went silver by the tons.
And warlords are encouraged in their careers,
While China is **carved**[3] up into many **spheres**[4].
When armies appear, poor peasants are **squeezed**[5],
Since their grain and beasts are always seized.
Now, Manager Wang, his reformer's **zeal**[6] burning,
Has turned his shop into a seat of learning.
With well-spoken students as lodgers in the place,
The teahouse has acquired a more educated face.
But pray to Heaven no **brutish**[7] soldiers come,
For **wrecking**[8] the teahouse is their idea of fun.
But I'd better not go on in this gloomy way,
I oug to wish him luck on his opening day.
With the crowd of well-wishers, I'll now **mingle**[9],
After all, I'm great at making up some jingle!
〔*Exit.*〕
〔*At his second entrance*〕

Silly Yang 〔*recites*〕
The old Yutai now looks brand new,
I hope all your dreams will come true.

Wang Lifa I'm not dealing with the likes of you today.
We're not opening till tomorrow.

金银财宝齐来到。
〔炮响。
您开张，他开炮，明天准唱《虫八蜡庙》。

王利发 去你的吧!
〔傻杨下。

第三幕 幕 前

大傻杨 树木老，叶儿稀，
人老毛腰把头低。
甭说我，混不了，
王掌柜的也过不好。
（他）钱也光，人也老，
身上剩了一件破棉袄。
自从那，日本兵，八年占据老北京。
人人苦，没法提，
不死也掉一层皮。
好八路，得人心，
一阵一阵杀退日本军。
盼星星，盼月亮，
盼到胜利大家有希望。
（哼）国民党，进北京，

① spoil /spɔil/ *v.* 破坏，腐坏

② sap /sæp/ *n.* 树液，汁液

③ mirth /mə:θ/ *n.* 欢乐，欢笑

Silly Yang Ah, tomorrow'll be beautiful, tomorrow'll be fine,

For you gold and silver, come rain come shine.

〔*Cannon-shots are heard.*〕

Cannons in the distance, something of a blow,

For your grand opening they may **spoil**① the show.

Wang Lifa Oh, get out of here!

〔*Exit Silly Yang.*〕

Act Three 〔*Before the curtain rises*〕

Silly Yang 〔*recites*〕

When trees are old, their **sap**② is spent,

When men are old, their backs are bent.

Needless to say, I'm done for altogether,

Even Manager Wang's at the end of his tether.

Worn down by age, his money gone,

His shabby winter jacket is all he's on.

The Japs held old Beijing for eig long years,

Those were the days of blood and tears.

For those who survived, life was hell on earth,

The Eigh Route Army's victories, the only source of **mirth**③.

Hoping against hope such days would soon be past,

Till the day came when the war was won at last.

横行霸道 一点不让日本兵。
王掌柜，委屈多，
跟我一样半死半活着。
老茶馆，破又烂，
想尽法子也没法办。
天可怜，地可怜，
就是官老爷有洋钱。
〔下。
〔王掌柜死后，傻杨再上，见小丁宝正在落泪。
小姑娘，别这样，
黑到头儿天会亮。
小姑娘，别发愁，
西山的泉水向东流。
苦水去，甜水来，
谁也不再做奴才。

Notes

① tyrant /'taiərənt/ *n.* 暴君

② disillusion /ˌdisi'luːʒən/ *v.* 醒悟，使幻想破灭

③ perk up 振作起来

④ dough /dəu/ *n.* ［美俚］钱，现钞

⑤ forlorn /fə'lɔːn/ *a.* 孤独的，悲惨的

⑥ haunt /hɔːnt/ *v.* 萦绕于心

⑦ yore /jɔː/ *n.* 〈书〉往昔，昔时

Then to old Beijing came the KMT!
As cruel a **tyrant**① as the Japs could ever be.
Poor old Wang, **disillusioned**② through and through,
Keeping alive is all that he can do.
His teahouse collapsing before his eyes,
Won't **perk up**③, no matter what he tries.
What in the heavens above or the earth below,
Can stop the officials from having all the **dough**④?

〔*Exit.*〕

〔*At the end, after Wang Lifa's death, Silly Yang enters once more, to find Ding Bao weeping.*〕

Now, little girl, don't be so **forlorn**⑤,
It's always darkest before the dawn.
Now, little girl, don't let it **haunt**⑥ you so,
Water from the Western Hills to the east shall flow.
That water is sweet, not the bitter stuff of **yore**⑦,
And all who drink it will be slaves no more.